Better Homes and Gardens®

Microwave Plus

On the cover:
Italian Pizza (see recipe, page 34)

BETTER HOMES AND GARDENS® BOOKS
Editor: Gerald M. Knox
Art Director: Ernest Shelton
Managing Editor: David A. Kirchner

Food and Nutrition Editor: Doris Eby
Department Head—Cook Books: Sharyl Heiken
Senior Food Editors: Rosemary C. Hutchinson, Elizabeth Woolever
Senior Associate Food Editor: Sandra Granseth
Associate Food Editors: Jill Burmeister, Linda Henry, Julia Malloy
Alethea Sparks, Marcia Stanley, Diane Yanney
Recipe Development Editor: Marion Viall
Test Kitchen Director: Sharon Stilwell
Test Kitchen Home Economists: Jean Brekke, Kay Cargill,
Marilyn Cornelius, Maryellyn Krantz, Marge Steenson

Associate Art Directors (Creative): Linda Ford, Neoma Alt West
Associate Art Director (Managing): Randall Yontz
Copy and Production Editors: Marsha Jahns,
Nancy Nowiszewski, Mary Helen Schiltz, David A. Walsh
Assistant Art Directors: Harijs Priekulis, Tom Wegner
Graphic Designers: Mike Burns, Trish Church-Podlasek,
Alisann Dixon, Mike Eagleton, Lynda Haupert, Deb Miner,
Lyne Neymeyer, Stan Sams, D. Greg Thompson,
Darla Whipple, Paul Zimmerman

Editor-in-Chief: Neil Kuehnl
Group Editorial Services Director: Duane L. Gregg

General Manager: Fred Stines
Director of Publishing: Robert B. Nelson
Director of Retail Marketing: Jamie Martin
Director of Direct Marketing: Arthur Heydendael

MICROWAVE PLUS
Editor: Julia Malloy
Copy and Production Editor: Mary Helen Schiltz
Graphic Designer: Harijs Priekulis

Our seal assures you that every recipe
in *Microwave Plus* has been tested in the
Better Homes and Gardens Test Kitchen. This means
that each recipe is practical and reliable, and meets
our high standards of taste appeal.

CONTENTS

microwave-plus cooking

The microwave oven turns out delicious foods that are fast and convenient, but it's certainly not the only appliance in your kitchen. If you attempted to do all of your food preparation in the microwave oven or in any single kitchen appliance, you could limit your success. Instead, consider the time and effort involved in preparing a recipe, as well as the food's appearance, then organize your cooking schedule around several appliances. If a microwave step requires too much attention, perhaps another appliance may be better

listed timing suggestions with each recipe. Remember that these times are approximate and that you will need to dovetail or work back and forth between recipes to complete all of the preparation steps. For example, for the breakfast menu on the following page, prepare the batter and start cooking the pancakes while the applesauce chills. During this same period, as work permits, cook the sausage links and make the breakfast nog. Before serving, heat the maple syrup in the microwave oven.

To make your schedule even easier and more flexible, we've indicated that you can prepare certain recipes the day before serving. The cocktail party menu pictured on these pages is a good example of this make-ahead feature. Turn to pages 84 and 85 for the menu and recipes for Orange-Coconut Dip with Fruit Dippers, Mustard-Glazed Meatballs, Sparkling Lime and Ginger Tea, Pork Egg Rolls, Creole-Style Party Mix, and Rosé Cooler.

6 COOKING PRINCIPLES

Cooking with the microwave oven plus other appliances makes good sense. But before you can make the most of "microwave-plus cooking," you will need to master some basic microwave techniques. You also should be familiar with the types of containers you can use in your counter-top microwave oven.

Microwave Containers

Whether cooking an entire recipe in the microwave or just a part of it, you need to remember that the types of containers you are able to use in the microwave oven are often quite different from those you would use in conventional cooking. However, you will probably find many containers appropriate for microwave cooking already in your cupboards.

Generally speaking, glass, paper, ceramics, and other containers that do not contain metal are microwave-safe. Avoid using metal, which is so basic to all conventional methods of cooking, because it reflects microwaves and causes arcing or sparks. Some microwave oven models do allow a limited use of metal, but you should consult your owner's manual to see if your model permits it.

Glass, ceramics, stoneware, and pottery lend themselves well to microwave cooking. Avoid using chipped or cracked dishes or utensils with metal trim or other parts. Check the dish manufacturer's instructions to see if you can transfer some of these materials from the microwave to the range top, oven, or broiler or grill.

Specific to the microwave oven is cooking with *paper products,* but be careful not to micro-cook paper for more than 4 minutes on high power. Use plastic-coated paper plates for heating moist foods, and non-coated paper plates to absorb moisture from

dry or crisp foods. Use white paper toweling to absorb moisture or fat.

Some *plastics* are manufactured especially for microwave use. Others can be used with caution. Use only heavy-duty plastics in the microwave oven because lightweight plastics or light plastic wrap may distort or melt. Do not use melamine as it is not transparent to microwaves. Avoid cooking foods that are high in fat or sugar in plastic since these will attract microwaves and cause high enough heat to melt the container. Microwave-safe plastic containers can be great for freezer-to-microwave oven cooking.

Microwave Dish Test

If you have checked your dish manufacturer's instructions and still are not sure if a glass, pottery, or china container is microwave-safe, you can perform the following test:

Pour ½ cup cold water into a glass measure. Set it inside or beside the dish you want to test. Micro-cook on high power for 1 minute. If the water is warm but the dish remains cool, the dish can be used for cooking. If the water is warm and the dish feels luke-warm, the dish is suitable for heating or reheating food. If the water stays cool while the dish becomes hot, do not use the dish in your microwave oven for any purpose.

This test is not satisfactory for plastic containers, since most plastics are transparent to microwaves. Distortion of some plastics is due to hot food, not microwave energy.

8 COOKING PRINCIPLES

Factors Affecting Microwave Cooking Timings

The *starting temperature* of a food has more effect on the timing in a microwave oven than in a conventional appliance. Starting to micro-cook a dish from room temperature can require about half as much time as starting it from the frozen state.

The *quantity or size and shape* of a food influences cooking speed, too. Two potatoes cook in almost double the time it takes for one potato. Foods of irregular sizes and shapes tend to cook unevenly. Some portions may overcook before the rest is done.

The *shape and size of the container* can also make a difference. Round dishes of even depth allow for the most even microwave penetration.

The *composition* of a food influences its cooking time. Dense foods such as roasts demand more time than porous foods such as muffins. Areas high in sugar or fat will cook more rapidly than other areas.

Microwave Cooking Techniques

Because microwaves penetrate certain areas in higher concentrations than others, foods tend to cook unevenly. To create an even temperature throughout and to speed up the cooking process, you will be utilizing several special microwave cooking techniques.

To distribute heat evenly, you may want to change the arrangement of a food. One method involves *stirring* sauces and mixtures several times during cooking. This brings cooler parts of the mixture from the center to the outside for exposure to microwaves. However, not all foods lend themselves to stirring, as in the case of layered casseroles or fish fillets. For these, you can *give the dish a half-turn* after part of the cooking time to allow microwaves to reach cooler portions. And for serving-size pieces

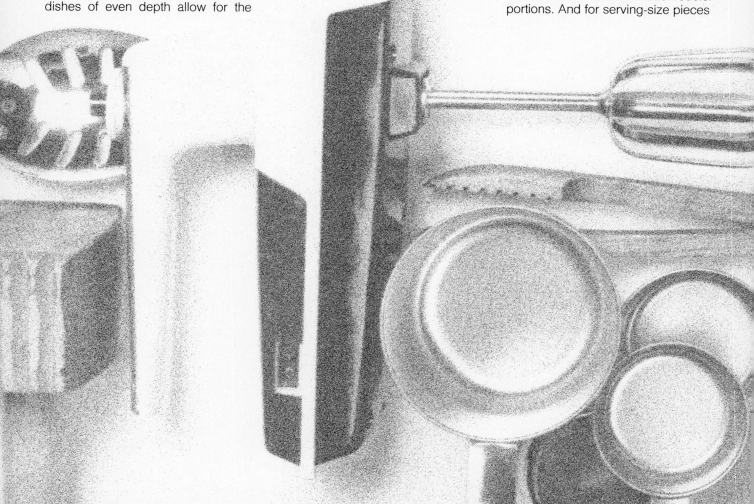

of meat and poultry, turn the pieces over or *rearrange* them with tongs, letting less-cooked portions face the outside of the dish.

If portions of a food are over-cooking and rearranging won't help, you may need to *shield* them from the microwaves.

Do this with small pieces of foil, but first check your owner's manual to see if you can safely use foil in your microwave oven.

To quicken the cooking process you will often trap steam by *covering* foods. If you use plastic wrap for this purpose, you should vent it by leaving a small area unsealed at the edge of the container to allow excess steam to escape. If a dish has its own micro-wave-safe lid, you can use it in place of vented plastic wrap.

Waxed paper often is used as a partial covering for foods to hold in steam and prevent spattering. Paper toweling also prevents foods from spattering. Choose undyed paper products, because dyes can leak onto the food. Look for products labeled as micorwave safe, then follow the manufacturer's instructions.

There are times you may not want to cover a dish at all. For instance, if you are micro-cooking a casserole with a crisp topping you will want to cook the dish uncovered to allow the moist steam to escape. And if you're trying to thicken a sauce that constantly needs stirring, you may not want to keep covering and uncovering the container every time you need to stir the sauce.

When cooking with the microwave oven you will find that it pays to under-cook foods slightly because they continue to cook while standing. This after-cooking is more pronounced in microwave cooking than in conventional cooking methods because of the high internal temperature that can build up within the food. Recipes in this book indicate how long a food should stand. Large or dense foods require the longest *standing times*.

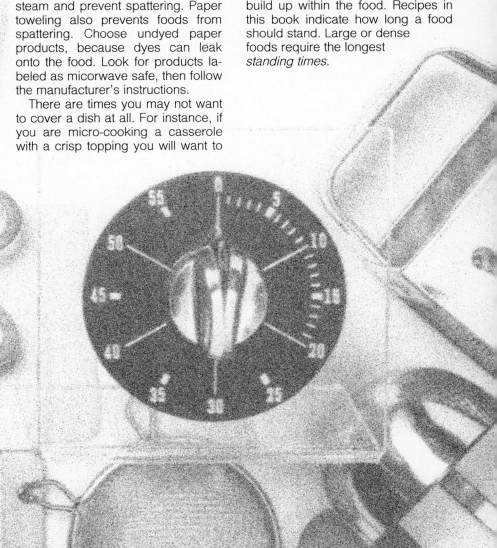

Once you are familiar with your microwave oven and basic microwave cooking techniques, you can begin to incorporate its potential timesaving value into your conventional recipes.

Start by sorting through your conventional recipes to select steps that you can do in the microwave oven. Keep in mind that microwaving is a moist cooking method. The easiest foods to micro-cook are those that are naturally moist, such as chicken, fish, ground beef, vegetables, and fruits. Other good choices include saucy main dishes, casseroles, and foods that are steamed, covered, or stirred during cooking. The microwave cooking steps may be as simple as sautéing chopped onion in butter to add to a casserole or cooking bacon slices for an omelet.

When converting parts of your own conventional recipes to microwave procedures, exercise care in choosing a cooking time. For accurate microwave timings, use this book and the following guidelines as a reference or a microwave recipe that has similar amounts of ingredients. If you can't locate a reliable source, try cutting the conventional cooking time to ⅓ or ¼ of the original time for cooking in the microwave oven. Test for doneness frequently, and if the food needs more cooking, increase the time in small increments.

In converting conventional cooking steps to microwave cooking, you may need to change the amounts of certain ingredients slightly. If a conventional recipe calls for fat to keep foods from sticking to the pan, you may be able to reduce or eliminate it because the moisture in the food itself prevents sticking. Since foods do retain their moisture content and little evaporation occurs, try cutting the amount of liquid in a conventional recipe to about ⅔ of its original volume. Just to be sure, check the food often during cooking to add more liquid if the food seems too dry. You may also want to reduce the amount of seasoning because microwaves enhance the natural flavor in foods.

Just as you can transfer conventional cooking steps to the microwave oven for speed and convenience, so can you add conventional steps to microwave recipes for practicality or appearance. For example, microwaved foods do not develop a dry, crisp crust. If this is an important feature of your recipe, you should probably bake it in your conventional oven. Or, if you do not like the color of a pie-crust baked in the microwave oven, use the microwave oven directions for the filling but bake the pie following timings from a similar conventional recipe.

The possibilities are endless. To start you on the right track, we've compiled a list of common microwave cooking steps you can apply to your conventional recipes. And although your microwave oven may offer variable-power cooking, for simplicity, recipes in this book require only the high or full-power setting. Look through the book and you'll find many creative ideas.

Cooking Ground Beef:
In a 2-quart nonmetal casserole stir together 1 pound ground beef and ½ cup chopped green pepper or onion. Micro-cook the mixture, uncovered, on high power about 5 minutes or till meat is no longer pink, stirring 3 times during cooking.

Cooking Bacon:
Place 4 slices of bacon on a paper plate between several layers of white paper toweling. Micro-cook on high power for 2½ to 3½ minutes or till the bacon is done.

Softening Unflavored Gelatin:
Sprinkle the unflavored gelatin over the cold liquid specified in the recipe. Let stand for 5 minutes. Micro-cook, uncovered, on high power till gelatin is dissolved, stirring once. Allow 45 to 60 seconds for ½ cup total mixture; 1½ to 1¾ minutes for 1 cup total mixture; and 2 to 2¼ minutes for 1½ cups total mixture.

Warming Dinner Rolls:
Place dinner rolls in a napkin-lined basket or on a nonmetal plate. Micro-cook, uncovered, on high power till warm. Allow 15 to 20 seconds for 1 or 2 dinner rolls; 30 to 50 seconds for 4 rolls; and 40 seconds to 1½ minutes for 6 rolls. For 3 or more rolls, give the basket or plate a half-turn once during cooking. Do not overcook the rolls, because breads can become tough if micro-cooked too long.

Making Plain Croutons:
Spread 4 cups ½-inch-thick bread cubes in a 12x7½x2-inch nonmetal baking dish. Micro-cook the bread, uncovered, on high power for 6 to 7 minutes or till crisp and dry, stirring after every 2 minutes.

Baking Potatoes:

Select baking potatoes of approximately the same size and shape (6 to 8 ounces each). Scrub potatoes and prick skins with a fork. Arrange potatoes in the microwave oven on paper toweling, leaving at least 1 inch between potatoes. Micro-cook, uncovered, on high power till potatoes are still slightly firm. Allow 3 to 5 minutes for 1 potato; 6 to 8 minutes for 2 potatoes; 10 to 13 minutes for 4 potatoes; and 15 to 18 minutes for 6 potatoes. When cooking two or more, rearrange potatoes and turn them over halfway through cooking. After micro-cooking the potatoes, wrap them in foil and let stand for 5 minutes to finish cooking.

Cooking Prepackaged Frozen Vegetables:

Unwrap one 9- or 10-ounce package of frozen vegetables or measure 1½ cups loose-pack frozen vegetables. Place the vegetables and 2 tablespoons water in a 1-quart nonmetal casserole. Cover and micro-cook on high power till vegetables are crisp-tender. Allow 5 to 7 minutes for frozen asparagus, broccoli, cauliflower, or brussels sprouts; or 4 to 6 minutes for whole kernel corn, mixed vegetables, or peas; 4 to 7 minutes for sliced carrots and cut green beans; and 7 to 9 minutes for spinach. Let stand, covered, for 3 minutes. Season with salt and butter or margarine, if desired.

Sautéing Onion in Butter:

In a small nonmetal bowl combine ½ cup chopped onion and 1 tablespoon butter or margarine. Micro-cook, covered, on high power for 2 to 3 minutes or till tender, stirring once or twice during cooking.

Peeling Tomatoes:

In a 2-cup glass measure micro-cook 1 cup water, uncovered, on high power for 1 to 2 minutes or till boiling. Spear tomato; dip into hot water about 12 seconds. Hold the tomato under cold running water till cool enough to handle; remove the peel.

Toasting Nuts:

Spread ¼ cup of desired nuts in a 9-inch nonmetal pie plate. Micro-cook the nuts, uncovered, on high power about 3 minutes or till toasted, stirring frequently.

Toasting Coconut:

In a 9-inch nonmetal pie plate spread ½ cup flaked coconut. Micro-cook, uncovered, on high power for 3 to 4 minutes or till golden. After 1½ minutes of micro-cooking, stir the coconut after every 30 seconds.

Melting Butter or Margarine:

In a small nonmetal bowl micro-cook butter or margarine, uncovered, on high power till melted. Allow 30 to 40 seconds for 2 tablespoons butter or margarine; 40 seconds to 1 minute for ¼ cup butter or margarine; and 1¼ to 2 minutes for ½ cup butter or margarine.

Melting Chocolate:

Place wrapped chocolate squares (1 ounce each) in the microwave oven with folded side of wrapper up. Micro-cook the wrapped squares on high power till melted. Allow about 2 minutes for 1 square and 2½ to 3 minutes for 2 squares. Lift the melted chocolate squares by the folded ends of the wrappers.

Melting Caramels:

Remove caramels from a 14-ounce package. Place the unwrapped caramels in a 1-quart nonmetal mixing bowl. Micro-cook the caramels, uncovered, on high power about 2½ minutes, stirring once during cooking.

Heating Ice Cream Topping:

Place the open glass jar of ice cream topping in the center of the microwave oven. Micro-cook, uncovered, on high power till heated through. Allow 45 to 60 seconds for a full 12-ounce jar of topping. Serve the warm topping immediately over ice cream.

Plumping Raisins or Currants:

In a nonmetal mixing bowl micro-cook 2 cups water, uncovered, on high power for 4 to 6 minutes or till boiling. Stir in 1 cup raisins or dried currants. Let stand for 5 minutes. Drain off excess water.

Making Instant Hot Beverages:

Fill 1 or 2 (6-ounce) nonmetal mugs with water. Micro-cook, uncovered, on high power till water is hot. Allow 1½ to 2 minutes for 1 mug and 3 to 4½ minutes for 2 mugs. Stir in desired beverage powder or mix.

Flaming:

To flame a sauce for a meat or dessert, place 2 to 4 tablespoons brandy or rum in a 1-cup glass measure. Micro-cook, uncovered, on high power for 15 to 20 seconds or till hot. Carefully ignite with a long match and pour over food.

MICROWAVE
PLUS RANGE TOP

Your range top and microwave oven work simultaneously to create elegant Shrimp Linguine (see recipe, page 22). While the pasta and the shrimp are cooking on the range top, your microwave oven is busy sautéing the mushroom mixture.

R ange-top cookery has certain advantages, as you will discover in this chapter.

The range top is great for deep-fat frying. It is also excellent for browning poultry and meat, not to mention crepes and pancakes.

Large volumes of food, such as sauces and soups, are often better suited to range-top cooking. Some of these foods require too much stirring when prepared in the microwave to justify its use.

You'll also want to use the range top for soups that need long simmering to blend flavors, and for sauces that you cook to reduce the liquid.

Pasta, rice, and dried beans take the same amount of time to rehydrate in the microwave oven as they do on the range top, so cook them conventionally and reserve the microwave oven for better uses.

A final note on "musts" for the range top. Always hard-cook eggs atop your range; eggs micro-cooked in their shells will explode when excess steam builds up within them.

PARSNIP BEEF ROLL

½ cup shredded parsnip
½ cup shredded carrot
⅓ cup finely chopped onion
¼ cup finely chopped green pepper
1 1½-pound beef round steak, cut ½ inch thick
1 tablespoon cooking oil
¼ cup brandy
1 tablespoon steak sauce
½ teaspoon instant beef bouillon granules
½ teaspoon dried tarragon, crushed
¼ teaspoon dried dillweed
2 medium parsnips, cut into strips
2 medium carrots, cut into strips
1 medium green pepper, cut into strips
1 medium onion, cut into wedges
½ cup whipping cream or light cream
1 tablespoon all-purpose flour

In a 1-quart nonmetal casserole combine the shredded parsnip and carrot, chopped onion and green pepper, and 2 tablespoons *water*. Cover and cook in the *microwave oven* on high power about 5 minutes or till tender; drain well.

Meanwhile, sprinkle steak with salt and pepper; pound till meat is ¼ inch thick. Spread the vegetable mixture over steak; roll up jelly-roll style. Tie securely.

On the *range top*, in a Dutch oven brown meat roll in hot oil. Stir in brandy, steak sauce, bouillon granules, tarragon, dillweed, ½ cup *water,* and ¼ teaspoon *pepper*. Cover and cook for 25 minutes.

Add the parsnip, carrot, and green pepper strips and the onion wedges; cover and cook for 20 to 25 minutes more or till tender, basting occasionally.

Transfer the meat to serving platter, reserving drippings in pan. Arrange the vegetables around meat; keep warm.

For sauce, skim fat from drippings. Stir together cream and flour; stir into drippings. On the *range top* cook and stir till thickened and bubbly. Cook and stir for 1 minute more. Pour over meat. Serves 6.

MEATBALLS IN ROSE-TOMATO SAUCE

2 cups medium noodles
1 beaten egg
1 medium apple, peeled and shredded (⅔ to ¾ cup)
¼ cup fine dry seasoned bread crumbs
¾ teaspoon salt
⅛ teaspoon garlic powder
⅛ teaspoon pepper
1 pound lean ground beef
1 tablespoon cooking oil
1 medium onion, cut into wedges
⅓ cup water
1 6-ounce can tomato paste
¼ cup rosé wine
¼ teaspoon dried rosemary, crushed
¼ teaspoon dried basil, crushed

On the *range top*, in a saucepan cook the noodles according to package directions; drain.

Meanwhile, in a mixing bowl combine the beaten egg, shredded apple, bread crumbs, salt, garlic powder, and pepper. Add the ground beef; mix well. Shape into 1½-inch meatballs.

On the *range top*, in a skillet cook the meatballs in hot cooking oil, *half* at a time, till brown on all sides; drain.

For sauce, place the onion wedges and water in a 1½-quart nonmetal casserole. In the *microwave oven* cook, covered, on high power for 1 to 2 minutes or till tender. Stir in the tomato paste, rosé wine, rosemary, and basil. Add the meatballs; cover and micro-cook on high about 5 minutes or till meatballs are done.

Serve the meatball mixture over the hot cooked noodles. Makes 4 servings.

BEEF-STUFFED SWEET POTATOES

- 4 **large sweet potatoes (about 8 ounces each)**
- 1 **pound ground beef**
- ¼ **cup sliced green onion**
- ½ **teaspoon salt**
- ¼ **teaspoon ground cinnamon**
- ⅛ **teaspoon pepper**
  Orange juice
- 1 **medium apple, peeled, cored, and chopped (1 cup)**
  Orange slices, halved (optional)
  Parsley sprigs (optional)

Wash, prick, and place the sweet potatoes on paper toweling in the *microwave oven*. Cook, uncovered, on high power for 8 to 13 minutes or till nearly done, rearranging once. Remove sweet potatoes; let stand for 3 minutes.

Meanwhile, on the *range top*, in a 10-inch skillet cook the ground beef and sliced green onion till meat is brown and onion is tender; drain off fat.

Cut a lengthwise slice from the top of each sweet potato. Discard the skins from the slices; reserve slices. Scoop out the centers of the potatoes, leaving a ¼-inch-thick shell. Reserve the centers; set the shells aside.

For filling, in a large mixing bowl combine the centers and the top slices of the potatoes. Beat in salt, cinnamon, pepper, and enough orange juice to make fluffy (about 2 tablespoons). Fold the meat mixture into the sweet potato mixture. Fold in the chopped apple. Season to taste with additional salt and pepper.

Spoon the filling into the sweet potato shells. Place the filled shells in a shallow nonmetal baking dish; cover loosely with clear plastic wrap or waxed paper. In the *microwave oven* cook on high power for 5 to 7 minutes or till heated through. Garnish with halved orange slices and sprigs of parsley, if desired. Makes 4 servings.

MOUSSAKA

- 1 **medium eggplant (1¼ pounds)**
- 1½ **pounds lean ground beef *or* lamb**
- ½ **cup finely chopped onion**
- 1 **clove garlic, minced**
- 1 **6-ounce can tomato paste**
- ½ **cup dry red wine**
- 1 **teaspoon ground cinnamon**
- ½ **teaspoon dried oregano, crushed**
- 3 **tablespoons butter *or* margarine**
- 3 **tablespoons all-purpose flour**
- ¼ **teaspoon ground nutmeg**
- 1½ **cups milk**
- 1 **beaten egg**
- ¼ **cup grated Parmesan cheese**
- 1 **tablespoon fine dry bread crumbs**

Slice the eggplant into ¼-inch-thick rounds; halve large slices. Place in a 10x6x2-inch nonmetal baking dish; add 2 tablespoons *water*. Cover and cook in the *microwave oven* on high power for 6 to 10 minutes or till done, rearranging once during cooking. Drain.

In a 2-quart nonmetal casserole combine meat, onion, and garlic. Micro-cook, covered, on high for 7 to 9 minutes or till meat is brown, stirring once. Drain off fat. Stir in tomato paste, wine, cinnamon, oregano, and ½ teaspoon *salt;* set aside.

For sauce, on the *range top* melt the butter or margarine in a medium saucepan; stir in flour, nutmeg, and ½ teaspoon *salt*. Add milk all at once. Cook and stir till thickened and bubbly. Cook and stir for 1 minute more. Gradually stir the hot mixture into egg. Stir in Parmesan cheese.

Sprinkle bread crumbs in the bottom of the 10x6x2-inch nonmetal baking dish; arrange *half* of the eggplant in dish. Top with meat mixture, then remaining eggplant slices. Pour sauce over all.

In the *microwave oven* cook, uncovered, on high power for 8 to 10 minutes or till heated through, giving the dish a half-turn once. Let stand 5 to 10 minutes before serving. Makes 8 to 10 servings.

PEPPER BEEF HEART

The beef heart is simmered on the range top to tenderize it for this saucy dish—

- 1½ **pounds beef heart (about ½ heart)**
- 1½ **cups beef broth**
- 1 **cup long grain rice**
- ¾ **cup chopped green pepper**
- ½ **cup bias-sliced celery**
- 2 **tablespoons soy sauce**
- 1 **tablespoon cornstarch**
- 1 **3-ounce can sliced mushrooms, drained**
- 2 **medium tomatoes, cut into wedges**

Remove and discard hard portions and fat from heart. Cut the meat into ½-inch pieces. In a medium saucepan combine meat and beef broth. Simmer, covered, on the *range top* about 45 minutes or till meat is nearly tender. Drain meat, reserving 1 cup beef broth.

Meanwhile, on the *range top* cook the rice according to package directions; keep warm.

Transfer the beef heart to a 1½-quart nonmetal casserole; add the reserved beef broth, the chopped green pepper, and celery. In the *microwave oven* cook, covered, on high power about 5 minutes or till the heart is done and the vegetables are crisp-tender.

Stir soy sauce into cornstarch; stir into casserole. Micro-cook, uncovered, on high for 3 to 4 minutes or till the mixture is thickened and bubbly, stirring after every minute.

Add the mushroom slices and tomato wedges; micro-cook, covered, on high about 1 minute more or till heated through. Serve over the hot cooked rice. Makes 6 to 8 servings.

PORK CHOPS WITH CASHEW PILAF

To help cook the pork chops evenly, first brown them slowly in a skillet—

- 1 **cup regular brown rice**
- 6 **pork chops, cut ¾ inch thick (2½ pounds total)**
  Garlic salt
  Salt
  Pepper
- ½ **cup coarsely chopped cashews**
- ½ **cup chopped celery**
- ¼ **cup finely chopped onion**
- 3 **tablespoons soy sauce**
- ¼ **teaspoon ground ginger**
- 1 **10¾-ounce can condensed cream of mushroom soup**
- ½ **cup dairy sour cream**
- ⅓ **cup milk**

On the *range top*, in a medium saucepan cook the brown rice according to package directions.

Meanwhile, trim fat from chops. On the *range top*, in a large skillet cook the fat till about 2 tablespoons drippings accumulate. Remove and discard the pieces of fat, reserving drippings. Cook the pork chops slowly in the hot drippings for 12 to 15 minutes. Season the meat with garlic salt, salt, and pepper.

In a mixing bowl combine the cooked brown rice, the cashews, celery, onion, soy sauce, and ginger. Spread the rice mixture in a 12x7½x2-inch nonmetal baking dish; arrange the chops atop. Cover with vented clear plastic wrap.

In the *microwave oven* cook on high power for 12 to 15 minutes or till the pork chops are tender and done throughout, rearranging chops twice during cooking (cut into the chop in several places to check that *no pink remains*).

For sauce, in a 4-cup glass measure combine the condensed cream of mushroom soup, the sour cream, and milk. Micro-cook on high, uncovered, about 2 minutes or till heated through, stirring after every 30 seconds. (*Do not boil.*) Serve the sauce over the pork chops and rice. Makes 6 servings.

CORN-FRIED PORK CHOPS

- 4 **pork chops, cut ½ inch thick (1½ pounds total)**
- ¼ **cup water**
  Salt
  Pepper
- ⅓ **cup cornmeal**
- ¼ **cup all-purpose flour**
- 2 **teaspoons chili powder**
- 1 **egg**
- ⅓ **cup milk**
- ½ **cup shortening *or* cooking oil**
- 1 **7¾-ounce can semi-condensed tomato soup**
- 2 **tablespoons prepared mustard**
- 1 **tablespoon vinegar**
- 1 **tablespoon butter *or* margarine**
  Green chili peppers (optional)

In a 12x7½x2-inch nonmetal baking dish place chops in the water; cover with vented clear plastic wrap. In the *microwave oven* cook on high power for 10 to 12 minutes or till chops are tender and done throughout (cut into chops in several places to make sure that *no pink remains*); give the dish a half-turn after every 5 minutes. Remove and drain the chops on paper toweling. Season with salt and pepper.

Meanwhile, in a mixing bowl stir together the cornmeal, flour, and chili powder. Combine the egg and milk; add to flour mixture and beat with a fork till smooth.

Dip the chops, one at a time, into the egg mixture to coat both sides evenly. On the *range top*, in a 12-inch skillet heat shortening or cooking oil to 350°. Fry chops for 2 to 3 minutes on each side or till golden brown. Drain on paper toweling. Keep warm.

Meanwhile, for sauce, in a 2-cup glass measure stir together the tomato soup, mustard, vinegar, and butter or margarine. In the *microwave oven* cook tomato mixture, covered, on high power for 1 to 2 minutes or till heated through and butter is melted. Serve the sauce over pork chops. Garnish with green chili peppers, if desired. Makes 4 servings.

PORK AND NOODLE CASSEROLE

Let the noodles cook on the range top while you prepare the pork mixture in the microwave oven—

- 4 **ounces medium noodles**
- 1 **pound ground pork**
- 1 **small onion, chopped (¼ cup)**
- 1 **16-ounce can stewed tomatoes**
- 1 **12-ounce can whole kernel corn, drained**
- 1 **6-ounce can tomato paste**
- 1 **teaspoon chili powder**
- ½ **teaspoon salt**
- ¼ **teaspoon garlic powder**
  Dash pepper
- 1 **cup shredded cheddar cheese (4 ounces)**

On the *range top* cook the noodles in boiling salted water according to package directions; drain.

Meanwhile, in a 2-quart nonmetal casserole combine the ground pork and chopped onion. In the *microwave oven* cook, covered, on high power about 5 minutes or till the meat is brown throughout and the onion is tender, stirring once during cooking. Drain off fat.

Add the *undrained* tomatoes, corn, tomato paste, chili powder, salt, garlic powder, and pepper to meat mixture; stir till combined. Add the cooked noodles; toss gently to mix.

Micro-cook the noodle mixture, uncovered, on high about 10 minutes or till heated through, stirring after 5 minutes. Sprinkle with the cheddar cheese. Cover and let stand about 5 minutes or till cheese is melted. Makes 6 servings.

16 PLUS RANGE TOP MAIN DISHES

CRISPY MANDARIN PORK

Pictured on pages 4 and 5—

Rice sticks *or* **long grain rice**
Shortening *or* **cooking oil for**
   deep-fat frying
½ **cup packaged biscuit mix**
¼ **cup cornstarch**
1 **tablespoon sesame seed**
1 **egg white**
2 **tablespoons soy sauce**
1 **pound boneless pork, cut into**
   ¾-inch pieces
1 **11-ounce can mandarin**
   orange sections
2 **medium carrots, thinly**
   bias-sliced
⅓ **cup catsup**
¼ **cup sugar**
2 **tablespoons vinegar**
1 **teaspoon instant chicken**
   bouillon granules
2 **medium green peppers, cut**
   into ¾-inch squares

On the *range top* fry rice sticks in hot oil (375°) about 5 seconds or till sticks puff and rise. Drain and keep warm. (Or, cook rice according to package directions.)

Stir together biscuit mix, *2 tablespoons* of the cornstarch, and sesame seed. Combine egg white, soy sauce, and ¼ cup *water;* add to dry ingredients. Stir in pork. On the *range top* fry pork, about 8 pieces at a time, in hot oil (365°) for 2 to 3 minutes. Drain and keep warm.

Meanwhile, for sauce, drain orange sections, reserving liquid. In a 4-cup glass add enough water to liquid to measure 1¼ cups. Add carrots. In the *microwave oven* cook, covered, on high power for 5 to 6 minutes or till crisp-tender.

For sauce, combine catsup, sugar, remaining cornstarch, vinegar, and bouillon granules. Add catsup mixture and green pepper to carrot mixture. Micro-cook, uncovered, on high for 4 to 5 minutes or till bubbly, stirring every minute. Stir in orange sections. Cover; micro-cook on high 1 minute. Serve pork and sauce over rice sticks or rice. Serves 4.

FRANK AND CHILI MANICOTTI

The microwave shortens the cooking time of this Mexican-style manicotti—

8 **manicotti shells**
6 **ounces Monterey Jack cheese**
1 **16-ounce package frankfurters**
   (8 frankfurters)
2 **15-ounce cans chili beans in**
   chili gravy
1 **10-ounce can tomatoes and**
   green chili peppers, drained
   and cut up

On the *range top*, in a Dutch oven cook the manicotti shells in boiling salted water according to package directions. Drain and set aside.

Meanwhile, shred about *two-thirds* of the Monterey Jack cheese (you should have about 1 cup); set aside. Cut the remaining cheese into 8 strips, each 3 to 4 inches long. Slit each frankfurter lengthwise to the center, making a pocket. Insert a strip of cheese into each frankfurter pocket. Place one cheese-stuffed frankfurter inside each cooked manicotti shell.

In a mixing bowl combine the chili beans in chili gravy and the drained tomatoes and chili peppers. Spoon *half* of the mixture (you should have about 2 cups) into the bottom of a 12x7½x2-inch nonmetal baking dish. Arrange the filled manicotti shells atop the chili mixture in dish; pour the remaining chili mixture over all.

Cover loosely with clear plastic wrap and cook in the *microwave oven* on high power about 10 minutes or till heated through, turning the dish twice during cooking. Uncover and sprinkle the reserved shredded cheese atop. Micro-cook on high, uncovered, for 1 to 2 minutes more or till the cheese is melted. Makes 4 or 5 servings.

BACON 'N' EGG MUFFIN STACKS

Keep the delicate sauce warm in a double boiler while reheating the muffin stacks—

6 **eggs**
6 **slices Canadian-style bacon,**
   cut ¼ inch thick
3 **English muffins, split and**
   toasted
3 **egg yolks**
½ **cup butter** *or* **margarine**
½ **teaspoon finely shredded**
   orange peel
2 **tablespoons orange juice**
   Dash ground red pepper

Place 6 eggs in saucepan; cover with cold water. On *range top* bring to boiling; reduce heat to just below simmering. Cover; cook for 15 minutes. Let cool. Remove shells; cut into wedges.

Place bacon slices between paper toweling on a paper plate. In the *microwave oven* cook on high power about 2 minutes or till heated through. Place one slice atop each muffin half; top each with the wedges of one hard-cooked egg.

For sauce, place egg yolks in a blender container or food processor bowl. Cover and blend or process about 5 seconds or till blended. In a 2-cup glass measure combine butter or margarine, orange peel, orange juice, and red pepper. Micro-cook, uncovered, about 1 minute or till butter or margarine is almost melted.

Through opening in lid of blender or food processor (or with blender lid slightly ajar), slowly pour butter mixture into container while blending or processing on high speed about 1½ minutes or till mixture is thickened and fluffy.

On the *range top* keep sauce warm in the top of a double boiler over hot (not boiling) water (upper pan should not touch water).

Meanwhile, place the muffin stacks on a paper plate. In the *microwave oven* cook, uncovered, on high power about 1½ minutes or till heated through. To serve, spoon some of the sauce over each muffin stack. Makes 6 servings.

HAM-ROMAINE ROLLS

Pictured on page 20—

¼ **cup long grain rice**
¼ **cup finely chopped onion**
1 **beaten egg**
2 **tablespoons milk**
1 **tablespoon horseradish mustard**
2 **cups finely chopped, fully cooked ham**
12 **large romaine leaves** *or* **cabbage leaves**
Horseradish Sauce
Paprika

On the *range top* cook rice according to package directions, *except* cook onion with rice. Combine egg, milk, and mustard. Stir in ham and the rice mixture.

Remove the stem end of heavy center vein from the bottom of each romaine or cabbage leaf, keeping each leaf in one piece. Place leaves in a 12x7½x2-inch nonmetal baking dish; cover with vented clear plastic wrap. In the *microwave oven* cook on high power for 3 to 5 minutes or till limp; drain.

Place 2 leaves together, overlapping the long edges slightly. Top with about ½ cup of the filling; fold in sides. Starting at the bottom, roll up, making sure the folded sides are included in the roll. Repeat with the remaining leaves and filling.

Place the rolls, seam side down, in the 12x7½x2-inch nonmetal baking dish. Micro-cook rolls, covered, on high about 10 minutes or till heated through.

Meanwhile, on the *range top* prepare Horseradish Sauce. Spoon *some* of the sauce over rolls. Sprinkle with paprika. Pass remaining sauce. Makes 6 servings.

Horseradish Sauce: On the *range top*, in a small saucepan heat 2 tablespoons *butter or margarine* till melted. Stir in 2 tablespoons *all-purpose flour*, 2 tablespoons *horseradish mustard,* and 1 teaspoon *instant chicken bouillon granules*. Add 1 cup *milk* all at once. Cook and stir till thickened and bubbly. Cook and stir for 1 minute more.

Filling and Rolling Romaine or Cabbage Rolls

With a sharp knife or kitchen scissors, cut lengthwise along both sides of the heavy center vein of each romaine or cabbage leaf, as shown, without cutting the leaf in half. Remove and discard the vein. The leaves will be easier to roll without this stiff center.

Place the long edges of two romaine or cabbage leaves together, overlapping the edges to strengthen the center of the roll. Place about ½ cup of the filling in the center where the leaves overlap, as shown.

Fold the long side edges of the leaves over the filling, as shown. Roll up carefully, starting at the cut portion of the leaves. Keep the sides folded over the filling while rolling to prevent it from leaking out of the roll. If desired, skewer the rolls closed with wooden picks.

QUICK-COOKED CHICKEN

Don't panic when a recipe calls for cooked chicken. Just micro-cook the amount you need. For 1 cup of cubed cooked chicken, arrange about 1 pound of chicken breasts in a 2-quart nonmetal casserole and add 1 tablespoon water. Cover and cook in the microwave oven on high power for 6 to 8 minutes, turning chicken over after 4 minutes. Cool slightly; remove and discard skin and bones. Cube the chicken.

CHICKEN AND MACARONI BAKE

- 1 2½- to 3-pound broiler-fryer chicken, cut up
- 1 7-ounce package (2½ cups) corkscrew macaroni
- 1 15½-ounce jar meatless spaghetti sauce
- ¼ cup dry white wine
  Paprika
- ¼ cup grated Parmesan cheese

Rinse chicken pieces; pat dry. On the *range top* cook macaroni according to package directions; drain.

In a 3-quart nonmetal casserole combine the macaroni, spaghetti sauce, and wine. Add chicken pieces, placing meatiest portions toward outside of dish. Sprinkle with paprika.

In the *microwave oven* cook the casserole, covered, on high power for 20 to 25 minutes or till chicken is tender, giving the dish a quarter-turn three times during cooking. Spoon off fat. Sprinkle with Parmesan cheese. Makes 6 servings.

CHICKEN WITH TURMERIC RICE

For an appetizing color, lightly brown the chicken before micro-cooking—

- 1 cup long grain rice
- ½ teaspoon ground turmeric
- 1 2½- to 3-pound broiler-fryer chicken, cut up
- 2 tablespoons cooking oil

- 1 8-ounce can pizza sauce
- ½ cup chopped onion
- ½ cup chopped celery
- 1 clove garlic, minced
- ¼ cup water
- 1 teaspoon salt
- ⅛ teaspoon pepper

On the *range top* cook rice according to package directions *except* add the turmeric before cooking.

Meanwhile, rinse chicken pieces; pat dry with paper toweling. On the *range top*, in a large skillet cook the chicken pieces in hot cooking oil for 10 to 15 minutes, turning pieces to brown evenly.

Arrange the chicken pieces in a 12x7½x2-inch nonmetal baking dish with meatiest portions toward the outside of dish. Combine the pizza sauce, chopped onion, chopped celery, garlic, water, salt, and pepper; pour over chicken.

Cover the dish with vented clear plastic wrap and cook in the *microwave oven* on high power for 10 to 15 minutes or till the chicken is tender, giving the dish a half-turn once during cooking. Spoon off fat from sauce, if necessary. Serve the chicken and sauce over the hot turmeric rice. Makes 6 servings.

RAISIN AND CHICKEN CURRY

- 1 cup long grain rice
- 1 2½- to 3-pound broiler-fryer chicken, cut up
- ¼ cup all-purpose flour
- 1 teaspoon salt
- ¼ teaspoon pepper
- 3 tablespoons cooking oil
- 1 medium onion, chopped (½ cup)
- 1 medium green pepper, chopped (½ cup)
- 1 clove garlic, minced
- 2 tablespoons water
- 1½ teaspoons curry powder
- 1 16-ounce can tomatoes, cut up
- ¼ cup raisins *or* dried currants

On the *range top* cook rice according to package directions.

Rinse chicken pieces; pat dry with paper toweling. In a plastic or paper bag combine flour, salt, and pepper. Add chicken pieces to bag, a few at a time, and shake to coat with flour mixture.

On the *range top*, in a skillet cook the chicken pieces in hot cooking oil for 10 to 15 minutes, turning the pieces to brown evenly; set aside.

In a 12x7½x2-inch nonmetal baking dish combine onion, green pepper, garlic, the water, and curry powder; cover with vented clear plastic wrap. In the *microwave oven* cook on high power about 2 minutes or till vegetables are crisp-tender. Stir in *undrained* tomatoes and raisins; add the chicken pieces, placing meatiest portions toward outside of dish.

Micro-cook, covered, on high for 10 to 15 minutes or till the chicken is tender, giving the dish a half-turn once during cooking. Spoon off fat from sauce, if necessary. Serve over the hot cooked rice. Makes 6 servings.

ROMAN-STYLE CHICKEN BREASTS

- 2 **whole medium chicken breasts, skinned and halved lengthwise**
- ¼ **cup all-purpose flour**
- ½ **teaspoon salt**
  Dash pepper
- 1 **tablespoon butter *or* margarine**
- ½ **cup chopped onion**
- 1 **clove garlic, minced**
- 1 **tablespoon butter *or* margarine**
- 2 **medium tomatoes, peeled and chopped (1½ cups)**
- ½ **cup fully cooked ham, cut into strips**
- ⅓ **cup dry white wine**
- ¼ **teaspoon dried rosemary, crushed**
- 1 **tablespoon cornstarch**
- 2 **tablespoons cold water**
  Green onion fans (optional)

Rinse chicken pieces; pat dry with paper toweling. In a plastic or paper bag combine flour, salt, and pepper. Add chicken pieces to bag, a few at a time, and shake to coat with flour mixture.

On the *range top*, in a skillet cook the chicken in 1 tablespoon butter or margarine for 8 to 10 minutes, turning pieces to brown evenly; set aside.

In a 12x7½x2-inch nonmetal baking dish combine onion, garlic, and 1 tablespoon butter or margarine; cover with vented clear plastic wrap. In the *microwave oven* cook on high power for 2 to 3 minutes or till onion is tender. Stir in chopped tomatoes, ham strips, wine, and rosemary; add chicken pieces. Micro-cook, covered, on high for 10 to 15 minutes or till chicken is tender, rearranging chicken pieces once. Transfer chicken to a serving platter, reserving tomato mixture in baking dish.

For sauce, stir cornstarch into the water; stir into the baking dish. Micro-cook, uncovered, on high for 2 to 4 minutes or till thickened and bubbly, stirring after every minute. Pour the sauce over the chicken. Garnish with green onion fans, if desired. Makes 4 servings.

CHICKEN AND WILD RICE PILAF

- 1 **6-ounce package regular long grain and wild rice mix**
- 3 **whole medium chicken breasts, skinned, halved lengthwise, and boned**
- 1 **tablespoon butter *or* margarine**
- 1 **10-ounce package frozen peas**
  Salt
  Pepper
- ¼ **cup pine nuts *or* slivered almonds, toasted**
- 2 **tablespoons dry sherry**

On the *range top*, in a saucepan cook the long grain and wild rice mix according to package directions.

Meanwhile, with a sharp knife cut the chicken breasts into ½-inch strips; set aside. Place the butter or margarine in a 12x7½x2-inch nonmetal baking dish. In the *microwave oven* cook, uncovered, on high power for 30 to 45 seconds or till butter is melted.

Add the chicken strips and frozen peas to melted butter or margarine in baking dish; toss to coat. Sprinkle with salt and pepper. Cover the dish with vented clear plastic wrap and micro-cook on high about 8 minutes or till chicken is done and peas are tender, stirring once during cooking.

Stir the pine nuts or toasted slivered almonds and dry sherry into the cooked rice mixture in the saucepan. Add the rice mixture to the chicken mixture in the baking dish; toss gently to mix. Micro-cook, covered, on high for 1 to 2 minutes more or till the mixture is heated through. Makes 6 servings.

HERBED CHICKEN ROLLS

- 2 **whole medium chicken breasts, skinned, halved lengthwise, and boned**
- ¼ **teaspoon dried basil, crushed**
- ⅛ **teaspoon garlic salt**
- ⅛ **teaspoon dried oregano, crushed**
  Dash pepper
- 4 **tablespoons stick butter *or* margarine, well chilled**
- 2 **tablespoons all-purpose flour**
- 1 **beaten egg**
- ⅓ **cup fine dry bread crumbs**
- 2 **tablespoons butter *or* margarine**

Place each chicken breast half between two pieces of clear plastic wrap. Pound with a meat mallet to ⅛-inch thickness, working from center to edges. Remove plastic wrap. Combine the basil, garlic salt, oregano, and pepper. Sprinkle one side of each chicken breast with some of the herb mixture.

Cut the 4 tablespoons stick butter or margarine lengthwise into four 2x1¼-inch sticks. Place 1 stick on the seasoned side of each chicken piece. Fold in the sides; roll up jelly-roll style. Seal the ends and fasten with wooden picks, if necessary.

Coat the chicken rolls with the flour; dip into the beaten egg, then into the bread crumbs to coat evenly. Cover and chill the rolls in the *refrigerator* for at least 1 hour.

On the *range top*, in a skillet cook the chicken rolls in the 2 tablespoons butter or margarine about 5 minutes or till brown on all sides. Transfer to an 8x8x2-inch nonmetal baking dish.

In the *microwave oven* cook chicken rolls, uncovered, on high power for 8 to 10 minutes or till done, giving the dish a half-turn once during cooking. Spoon the drippings over rolls. Makes 4 servings.

BROCCOLI AND FISH MOUSSE

1½ **pounds fresh *or* frozen fish fillets (individually frozen)**
2 **cups chopped fresh broccoli *or* one 10-ounce package frozen chopped broccoli**
1 **medium onion, chopped**
2 **tablespoons water**
¼ **teaspoon dried tarragon, crushed**
3 **eggs**
⅓ **cup dairy sour cream**
¼ **cup grated Parmesan cheese**
⅛ **teaspoon pepper**
½ **cup fine dry bread crumbs**

¼ **cup sliced green onion**
2 **tablespoons butter *or* margarine**
2 **tablespoons all-purpose flour**
1¼ **cups milk**
½ **cup shredded Swiss cheese**
1 **2½-ounce jar sliced mushrooms, drained**
1½ **cups frozen crinkle-cut carrots (optional)**
2 **tablespoons water (optional)**

Thaw fish, if frozen. In a 1½-quart nonmetal casserole combine the broccoli, onion, 2 tablespoons water, and tarragon. In the *microwave oven* cook, covered, on high power for 5 to 7 minutes or till the broccoli is crisp-tender, stirring once. Let stand, covered, for 3 minutes. Drain and cool slightly.

In a blender container or food processor bowl combine the cooked broccoli mixture, the eggs, sour cream, Parmesan cheese, and pepper. Cover and blend or process till the mixture is smooth, scraping the sides of the container with a spatula as necessary.

Finely chop *one-third* of the fresh or thawed fish. Stir chopped fish and dry bread crumbs into broccoli mixture. Cut remaining fish fillets into strips about 2 inches wide and 6 to 8 inches long.

To assemble, lay the fish strips in a greased 5-cup nonmetal mold at even intervals; overlap strips as necessary, letting ends hang over edges of mold. Carefully spoon the fish-broccoli mixture into the mold. Smooth top of broccoli mixture. Fold the hanging ends of fillets over the broccoli mixture.

Place the filled mold in a 12x7½x2-inch nonmetal baking dish. Add hot water to the baking dish to come halfway up the sides of the mold. In the *microwave oven* cook, uncovered, on high power about 10 minutes or till a knife inserted in the mixture near the center of the mold comes out clean, giving the dish a half-turn after 5 minutes.

Remove the filled mold from the baking dish of water. Let stand upright for 10 minutes. To drain off excess liquid, place a wire rack over mold; invert the mold over a pan (do not unmold). After draining, unmold the mousse onto a serving platter. Remove any excess liquid from platter using paper toweling.

Meanwhile, prepare the sauce on the *range top*. In a small saucepan cook green onion in butter or margarine till the onion is tender but not brown. Stir the flour into the onion mixture. Add the milk all at once. Cook and stir over medium heat till thickened and bubbly. Cook and stir for 1 minute more. Add the shredded Swiss cheese to the hot mixture, stirring till cheese is melted. Stir in the sliced mushrooms. Cook and stir over low heat till heated through.

If desired, prepare carrots for garnish. To cook carrots in the *microwave oven,* place the frozen carrots in a 1-quart nonmetal casserole; add 2 tablespoons water. Cover and cook on high power for 4 to 6 minutes or till carrots are tender, stirring once.

To serve, spoon *some* of the sauce over or around the mousse; pass the remaining sauce. Arrange the cooked carrot slices around the mousse, if desired. Makes 8 servings.

SOLE PATTIES PAPRIKASH

½ **cup long grain rice**
1 **pound fresh *or* frozen sole fillets**
2 **beaten eggs**
¾ **cup fine dry bread crumbs**
3 **tablespoons snipped parsley**
1 **tablespoon grated onion**
½ **teaspoon grated gingerroot**
2 **tablespoons cooking oil**
1 **tablespoon butter *or* margarine**
1 **tablespoon all-purpose flour**
1 **teaspoon paprika**
⅓ **cup light cream *or* milk**
2 **tablespoons dry white wine**

On the *range top* cook rice according to the package directions.

To thaw frozen fish, place the fish in a 10x6x2-inch nonmetal baking dish; cover with vented clear plastic wrap. In the *microwave oven* cook on high power about 2 minutes or till thawed, separating and turning fillets during cooking.

In the 10x6x2-inch baking dish micro-cook the fresh or thawed fish, covered, on high for 5 to 7 minutes or till fish flakes easily. Drain and flake.

Combine eggs, *¼ cup* of the bread crumbs, *2 tablespoons* of the parsley, the onion, gingerroot, and ¼ teaspoon *salt*. Stir in cooked rice and fish. Using about *⅓ cup* mixture for *each,* shape into eight ¾-inch-thick patties. (If necessary, chill before shaping.) Coat the patties with remaining bread crumbs. On the *range top* cook the patties in hot cooking oil for 6 minutes on each side or till golden.

Meanwhile, prepare sauce in the *microwave oven*. In a 4-cup glass measure micro-cook butter or margarine, uncovered, on high power about 30 seconds or till melted. Stir in flour and paprika. Add cream or milk all at once. Micro-cook, uncovered, on high about 1½ minutes or till thickened and bubbly, stirring after every 30 seconds. Stir in wine, remaining parsley, and ¼ cup *water*. Micro-cook, uncovered, on high about ½ to 1 minute more or till heated through. Serve the sauce over patties. Makes 4 servings.

Broccoli and Fish Mousse,
Ham-Romaine Rolls (see recipe, page 17)

TUNA AND CHEESE MANICOTTI

8 manicotti shells
3 small carrots, sliced (1 cup)
½ cup chopped onion
½ cup chopped celery
2 tablespoons water
1 beaten egg
1 9¼-ounce can tuna, drained and flaked
1 cup cream-style cottage cheese, well drained
¼ teaspoon lemon pepper
1¼ cups milk
2 tablespoons all-purpose flour
½ cup shredded process Swiss cheese (2 ounces)
½ cup sliced pitted ripe olives
Parsley sprigs (optional)

On the *range top* cook the manicotti shells according to package directions; drain well.

Meanwhile, in a 1-quart nonmetal casserole combine the carrot slices, onion, celery, and the water. In the *microwave oven* cook the vegetables, covered, on high power for 5 to 7 minutes or till tender, stirring once. Let stand for 3 minutes; drain well.

For filling, add the beaten egg, tuna, cottage cheese, and lemon pepper to *half* of the cooked vegetables. Spoon about ⅓ cup of the filling into *each* manicotti shell. Arrange filled shells in a 12x7½x2-inch nonmetal baking dish.

Prepare the sauce on the *range top.* In a saucepan stir together the milk and flour. Cook and stir over medium heat till thickened and bubbly. Cook and stir for 1 minute more. Add the shredded cheese, stirring till melted. Stir in the remaining cooked vegetables and sliced olives.

Pour the sauce over the filled manicotti shells in the baking dish; cover with vented clear plastic wrap. In the *microwave oven* cook on high power about 8 minutes or till heated through. Garnish manicotti with sprigs of parsley, if desired. Makes 4 servings.

CAPE COD PASTA

1 pound fresh *or* frozen fish fillets
1 cup frozen cut green beans
1 medium carrot, cut into ½-inch-thick slices (½ cup)
¾ cup water
½ cup dry white wine *or* water
¼ cup chopped onion
¼ cup sliced celery
5 whole black peppercorns, cracked
½ teaspoon salt
6 ounces spinach noodles
½ cup plain yogurt
3 tablespoons all-purpose flour
½ teaspoon dried tarragon, crushed
¼ teaspoon dried basil, crushed
½ cup milk
1 6½-ounce can minced clams, drained
Tomato wedges (optional)

Thaw fish, if frozen. Cut fresh or thawed fish into 1-inch cubes.

In a 2-quart nonmetal casserole combine beans, carrot, water, wine or water, onion, celery, peppercorns, and salt. In the *microwave oven* cook, covered, on high power for 5 to 6 minutes or till boiling. Stir in the fish cubes. Cover and micro-cook on high for 5 to 7 minutes more or till fish flakes easily when tested with a fork, stirring once. Drain fish and vegetables, reserving broth. Strain reserved broth.

Meanwhile, on the *range top* cook the spinach noodles according to package directions; drain.

For sauce, in a 3-quart saucepan stir together yogurt, flour, tarragon, and basil. Measure reserved fish broth; add water, if necessary, to make 1 cup liquid. Add reserved liquid to yogurt mixture; stir in milk. On the *range top* cook and stir till thickened and bubbly. Cook and stir for 1 minute more. Stir in clams and fish and vegetables; heat through. Season to taste with salt and pepper.

Place noodles in a serving dish; top with tomato wedges, if desired. Spoon the clam sauce atop. Makes 6 servings.

SHRIMP LINGUINE

Pictured on page 12—

6 ounces linguine
1 pound fresh *or* frozen shrimp in shells
1 cup sliced fresh mushrooms
⅓ cup butter *or* margarine
¼ cup sliced green onion
2 cloves garlic, minced
¼ cup grated Parmesan cheese
2 tablespoons snipped parsley
2 tablespoons dry white wine
½ teaspoon dried basil, crushed
⅛ teaspoon pepper
Grated Parmesan cheese

On the *range top* cook linguine in a large amount of boiling salted water according to package directions; drain.

On the *range top,* in a saucepan cook shrimp in boiling salted water for 1 to 3 minutes or till the shrimp turn pink. Drain. Carefully, remove the shell from each shrimp, leaving the tail intact. Devein the shrimp, if desired. (You should have about 2 cups cooked shrimp.)

Meanwhile, in a large nonmetal mixing bowl combine the sliced mushrooms, butter or margarine, green onion, and garlic; cover with vented clear plastic wrap. In the *microwave oven* cook on high power for 2 to 3 minutes or till green onion is tender. Stir in the cooked shrimp, the ¼ cup grated Parmesan cheese, parsley, wine, basil, and pepper. Micro-cook the mixture, uncovered, on high about 30 seconds more or till heated through.

Add drained linguine to shrimp mixture; toss gently to mix. Serve immediately. Pass additional Parmesan cheese, if desired. Makes 4 servings.

SHRIMP FLORENTINE

1 10-ounce package frozen
   chopped spinach
2 tablespoons water
¼ cup chopped onion
2 tablespoons butter *or*
   margarine
¼ teaspoon salt
⅛ teaspoon ground nutmeg
2 6-ounce packages frozen
   cooked shrimp, thawed and
   drained
¼ cup butter *or* margarine
3 tablespoons all-purpose flour
⅛ teaspoon garlic powder
⅔ cup chicken broth
½ cup light cream *or* milk
1 tablespoon lemon juice
⅓ cup slivered almonds, toasted
2 tablespoons grated Parmesan
   cheese

In a 1-quart nonmetal casserole combine spinach and water. Cover and cook in the *microwave oven* on high power for 7 to 9 minutes, stirring once. Let stand, covered, for 3 minutes. Drain spinach well, squeezing out excess liquid.

In a 10x6x2-inch nonmetal baking dish combine the onion and the 2 tablespoons butter or margarine; cover with vented clear plastic wrap. In the *microwave oven* cook on high power about 1½ minutes or till onion is tender. Stir in the drained spinach, salt, and nutmeg. Arrange the thawed shrimp atop.

On the *range top*, in a medium saucepan melt the ¼ cup butter or margarine; stir in the flour and garlic powder. Add the chicken broth and light cream all at once. Cook and stir till thickened and bubbly. Cook and stir for 1 minute more. Remove from heat. Stir in lemon juice.

Pour the mixture over the shrimp and spinach in baking dish, covering evenly. Combine the slivered almonds and Parmesan cheese; sprinkle atop.

In the *microwave oven* cook, uncovered, on high power for 4 to 5 minutes or till heated through, giving dish a half-turn once during cooking. Makes 4 servings.

GREEN BEAN FRENCH OMELETS

1 cup frozen cut green beans
2 tablespoons water
2 tablespoons sliced almonds
1 tablespoon butter *or* margarine
¼ teaspoon dried dillweed
   French Omelets
¼ cup shredded Swiss cheese

For filling, place the green beans and the water in a 1-quart nonmetal casserole. Cover and cook in the *microwave oven* on high power about 4 minutes. Let stand, covered, for 3 minutes; drain.

In the same casserole combine the drained beans, sliced almonds, butter or margarine, and dillweed. Micro-cook, covered, on high about 1 minute or till the butter is melted.

Meanwhile, on the *range top* prepare French Omelets. Pour *half* of the filling along center of *one* omelet; overlap sides of omelet over filling. Tilt skillet, then invert to roll the omelet out onto a warm serving plate. Repeat with the remaining omelet and filling. Top with the shredded Swiss cheese. Makes 2 servings.

French Omelets: In a small mixing bowl beat together 4 *eggs*, 2 tablespoons *water*, ¼ teaspoon *salt*, and ⅛ teaspoon *pepper* with a fork till mixture is blended but not frothy.

On the *range top*, in an 8-inch skillet with flared sides heat 1 tablespoon *butter or margarine* till it sizzles and browns slightly. Lift and tilt skillet to coat sides.

Pour in *half* of the egg mixture (about ½ cup); cook over medium heat. As eggs set, run a spatula around edge of the skillet, lifting the eggs to allow the uncooked portion to flow underneath. When eggs are set but still shiny, remove the skillet from heat. Fill as directed in recipe. Repeat with 1 tablespoon more *butter or margarine* and the remaining egg mixture.

POACHED EGGS WITH CAULIFLOWER SAUCE

The cauliflower thickens the sauce, eliminating the need for constant stirring—

1 10-ounce package frozen
   cauliflower
¼ cup water
   Milk (about 1 cup)
2 teaspoons instant chicken
   bouillon granules
¼ teaspoon dried basil, crushed
   Dash pepper
¼ cup shredded Swiss cheese
   (1 ounce)
1 tablespoon snipped parsley
12 eggs
6 English muffins, split and toasted

In a 1-quart nonmetal casserole combine cauliflower and the water. Cover and cook in the *microwave oven* on high power for 8 to 10 minutes or till very tender. Drain, reserving cooking liquid.

Measure cooking liquid; add enough milk to make 1 cup. In a blender container or food processor bowl combine the cooked cauliflower, milk mixture, bouillon granules, basil, and pepper. Cover and blend or process till smooth.

Return the blended mixture to the casserole. Stir in shredded Swiss cheese and the parsley; micro-cook, uncovered, about 1½ minutes more or till cheese is melted and mixture is heated through.

Meanwhile, to poach the eggs, lightly grease a 10-inch skillet. On the *range top* add enough water to half-fill the skillet; bring to boiling. Reduce heat to simmer. Break one egg into a small dish. Carefully slide egg into water, holding lip of dish as close to water as possible. Repeat with 3 more eggs. Simmer, uncovered, for 3 to 5 minutes or to desired doneness. Lift out with a slotted spoon. Poach the remaining eggs, 4 at a time.

To serve, place each poached egg atop one English muffin half. Pour the cauliflower sauce atop. Makes 6 servings.

COOKING DRY BEANS

To rehydrate, soak dry beans first, then cook them in a large amount of water. You will find it simpler to simmer the beans on the range top rather than cook them in your microwave oven. Because of their large dense volume, they would take a long time to micro-cook and would require frequent stirring during cooking.

MACARONI AND CHEESE

1½ **cups elbow macaroni**
2 **tablespoons butter *or* margarine**
2 **tablespoons all-purpose flour**
¾ **teaspoon salt**
  Dash pepper
2 **cups milk**
1½ **cups shredded cheddar cheese *or* shredded American cheese (6 ounces)**

On the *range top* cook macaroni according to package directions; drain.

In a 1½-quart nonmetal casserole cook butter or margarine, uncovered, in the *microwave oven* on high power for 30 to 40 seconds or till melted. Stir in the flour, salt, and pepper. Add milk all at once. Micro-cook, uncovered, on high for 6 to 7 minutes or till thickened and bubbly, stirring after every minute.

Add *1 cup* of the shredded cheddar or American cheese to the thickened mixture, stirring till cheese is melted. Stir in the cooked macaroni. Micro-cook, uncovered, on high for 7 to 8 minutes or till heated through, giving the casserole a half-turn once during cooking. Sprinkle the remaining shredded cheese atop. Makes 6 servings.

CHILI-SAUCED LIMA BEANS

2 **cups dry lima beans (12 ounces)**
4 **ounces salt pork, cut into ½-inch cubes**
1 **medium onion, chopped**
1 **clove garlic, minced**
2 **tablespoons butter *or* margarine**
1 **10¾-ounce can condensed tomato soup**
2 **tablespoons vinegar**
1 **tablespoon brown sugar**
1 **teaspoon prepared mustard**
1 **teaspoon Worcestershire sauce**
½ **teaspoon chili powder**

Rinse beans. On the *range top,* in a 4½-quart Dutch oven or large saucepan combine beans and 6 cups *water;* bring to boiling. Reduce heat; simmer, uncovered, for 2 minutes. Remove from heat. Cover and let stand for 1 hour. (*Or,* soak the beans in water overnight in a covered pan.) Drain beans and rinse.

On the *range top,* in the same Dutch oven or saucepan combine the rinsed beans and 6 cups more *water.* Add salt pork to beans. Cover and bring to boiling. Reduce heat; simmer for 1¼ to 1½ hours or till beans are tender. Drain the beans and set aside.

In the *microwave oven,* in a 2-quart nonmetal casserole or bean pot cook onion and garlic in butter or margarine, covered, on high power for 3 to 4 minutes or till tender. Stir in ¾ cup *water,* condensed tomato soup, vinegar, brown sugar, prepared mustard, Worcestershire sauce, and chili powder. Stir in the drained beans. Micro-cook, uncovered, on high about 20 minutes or till the mixture is heated through, stirring after every 5 minutes. Makes 8 servings.

PINTO BEAN AND BACON SOUP

Sprinkle some cheddar cheese atop each serving—

1¼ **cups dry pinto beans**
½ **cup brown rice**
3 **slices bacon, chopped**
2 **medium onions, chopped (1 cup)**
2 **cloves garlic, minced**
1 **16-ounce can tomatoes, cut up**
2 **teaspoons instant beef bouillon granules**
1 **teaspoon salt**
½ **teaspoon paprika**
¼ **teaspoon pepper**

Rinse beans. On the *range top,* in a 5-quart Dutch oven or kettle combine beans and 3 cups *water;* bring to boiling. Reduce heat; simmer, uncovered, for 2 minutes. Remove from heat. Cover and let stand for 1 hour. (*Or,* soak beans in water overnight in a covered pan.) Drain beans and rinse.

On the *range top,* in the same Dutch oven or kettle combine rinsed beans and 3 cups more *water.* Bring to boiling; reduce heat. Simmer, covered, about 2 hours or till beans are tender.

Meanwhile, on the *range top* cook the brown rice in a saucepan according to package directions.

In the *microwave oven,* in a 3-quart nonmetal casserole cook bacon, covered, on high power about 3 minutes or till almost crisp. Add the onion and garlic. Micro-cook, covered, on high for 2 to 3 minutes or till vegetables are tender.

Stir in the *undrained* cooked pinto beans, cooked brown rice, *undrained* tomatoes, beef bouillon granules, salt, paprika, and pepper. Add 2 cups more *water* and micro-cook, covered, on high about 15 minutes more or till heated through, stirring occasionally during cooking. Makes 8 servings.

ASPARAGUS WITH HERB SAUCE

The delicate orange-flavored sauce requires constant attention while thickening on the range top—

   1 **pound fresh asparagus** *or* **two 8-ounce packages frozen asparagus spears**
   2 **tablespoons water**
   ¼ **cup butter** *or* **margarine, softened**
   2 **beaten egg yolks**
   ¼ **cup plain yogurt**
   1½ **teaspoons all-purpose flour**
   ⅛ **teaspoon dried thyme, crushed**
   ⅛ **teaspoon dried basil, crushed**
      Dash salt
      Dash white pepper

   Place the fresh or frozen asparagus spears in a 12x7½x2-inch nonmetal baking dish; add the water. Cover tightly with vented clear plastic wrap and cook in the *microwave oven* on high power for 5½ to 9 minutes for fresh asparagus or 5½ to 7 minutes for frozen asparagus, giving the dish a half-turn once during cooking. Let stand, covered, for 3 to 5 minutes or till tender. Drain.
   Meanwhile, divide the butter or margarine into three portions. In the top of a small double boiler combine the egg yolks and *1 portion* of the butter or margarine. Place on the *range top* over boiling water (upper pan should not touch water). Cook and stir over low heat till butter is melted. Add another portion of the butter and continue stirring. As mixture thickens and the butter melts, add the remaining butter or margarine, stirring constantly. When butter is melted, remove from heat.
   Combine yogurt, flour, thyme, basil, salt, and white pepper. Stir into the egg yolk mixture. Place on the *range top* over boiling water (upper pan should not touch water). Cook and stir over low heat about 7 minutes or till thickened. Spoon the sauce over asparagus. Makes 6 servings.

Making Herb Sauce in the Double Boiler

After the first portion of butter or margarine melts, add the second portion and continue stirring with a wire whisk, as shown. As the butter or margarine melts, it forms fat globules that are held in suspension by the egg yolks. At this stage, the consistency of the sauce should be slightly thickened.

After adding the yogurt mixture, replace the top pan over boiling water (upper pan should not touch water). Heat the mixture, stirring constantly, about 7 minutes or till thickened. Remove from heat immediately. The sauce should be thick but pourable, as shown.
If the sauce curdles after thickening, immediately beat in 1 to 2 tablespoons boiling water.

26 PLUS RANGE TOP
SIDE DISHES

REHEATING LEFTOVER RICE

If you have some leftover cooked rice, store it in the refrigerator for up to 4 days.

To reheat the rice in your microwave oven, place 1 cup of chilled rice in a nonmetal mixing bowl. Cover the bowl with vented clear plastic wrap and micro-cook on high power about 1 minute or till heated through. Stir the rice gently with a fork to fluff.

ORANGE-BASIL RICE

2 cups water
1 cup long grain rice
2 teaspoons instant chicken bouillon granules
¼ cup finely chopped onion
3 tablespoons butter *or* margarine
1 clove garlic, minced
¼ teaspoon finely shredded orange peel
1 tablespoon orange juice
¼ teaspoon dried basil, crushed
⅛ teaspoon pepper

On the *range top*, in a saucepan combine the water, uncooked rice, and chicken bouillon granules. Bring to boiling; reduce heat. Cover and simmer for 15 to 20 minutes or just till rice is tender.

Meanwhile, in a 2-cup glass measure combine the onion, butter or margarine, and garlic; cover with vented clear plastic wrap. In the *microwave oven* cook on high power about 2 minutes or till the onion is tender. Stir in the orange peel, orange juice, basil, and pepper. Micro-cook on high about 30 seconds more.

Stir the orange-basil mixture into the cooked rice. Makes 6 servings.

LINGUINE WITH CLAM SAUCE

6 ounces green *or* white linguine
2 6½-ounce cans minced clams
2 tablespoons butter *or* margarine
1 large clove garlic, minced
2 tablespoons dry white wine Dash pepper
¼ cup snipped parsley
¼ cup grated Parmesan cheese Grated Parmesan cheese (optional)

On the *range top*, in a large saucepan cook the green or white linguine according to package directions; drain.

Meanwhile, drain the clams, reserving 2 tablespoons liquid. Set aside.

In a 2-cup glass measure combine the butter or margarine and minced garlic. In the *microwave oven* cook, uncovered, on high power for 40 seconds.

Stir the reserved clam liquid, dry white wine, and pepper into garlic; cover with vented clear plastic wrap. Micro-cook on high about 1 minute or till the mixture is boiling.

Stir the drained minced clams into the hot mixture. Micro-cook, covered, on high for 30 to 45 seconds more or till heated through.

In a serving bowl combine the clam mixture, cooked linguine, snipped parsley, and ¼ cup Parmesan cheese. Toss gently till the pasta is well coated. If desired, pass additional Parmesan cheese. Makes 4 side-dish servings.

BROCCOLI-RICE CASSEROLE

For this family favorite, combine some of the ingredients in the microwave oven while the rice cooks on the range top—

1½ cups long grain *or* brown rice
1 10-ounce package frozen chopped broccoli
2 tablespoons water
1 stalk celery, chopped (½ cup)
¼ cup chopped onion
2 tablespoons butter *or* margarine
1 10¾-ounce can condensed cream of mushroom soup
1 8-ounce jar cheese spread
¼ cup milk

On the *range top*, in a covered saucepan cook the long grain rice or brown rice according to package directions; set aside.

Meanwhile, combine frozen broccoli and the water in a 2-quart nonmetal casserole. In the *microwave oven* cook, covered, on high power for 5 to 7 minutes. Let stand, covered, for 3 minutes or till the broccoli is tender; drain well and set the broccoli aside.

In the same casserole combine the chopped celery, chopped onion, and butter or margarine. Micro-cook the mixture, covered, on high about 2 minutes or till the onion is tender. Stir in the condensed cream of mushroom soup, the cheese spread, and milk. Stir in the cooked long grain or brown rice and broccoli.

Micro-cook the broccoli-rice mixture, uncovered, on high for 8 to 10 minutes or till heated through, stirring the mixture once or twice during cooking. Makes 12 to 14 servings.

EGGNOG DOUGHNUTS

3⅓ cups all-purpose flour
  2 packages active dry yeast
  ¾ teaspoon ground nutmeg
  1 cup dairy *or* canned eggnog
  ⅓ cup sugar
  ¼ cup butter *or* margarine
  ½ teaspoon salt
  2 eggs
    Eggnog Glaze
    Cooking oil for deep-fat frying

In a large mixer bowl combine *2 cups* of the flour, yeast, and nutmeg.

In a 4-cup glass measure combine the eggnog, sugar, butter or margarine, and salt. In the *microwave oven* cook, uncovered, on high power for 30 to 60 seconds or just till warm (115° to 120°) and butter or margarine is almost melted, stirring once during cooking.

Add the warm eggnog mixture to the flour mixture in the mixer bowl; add eggs. Beat on low speed of electric mixer for ½ minute, scraping sides of bowl constantly. Beat for 3 minutes on high speed. Stir in as much of the remaining flour as you can mix in with a spoon to make a soft dough. Shape into a ball. Place dough in a lightly greased bowl; turn once to grease surface. Cover and chill the dough for 3 hours or overnight.

Punch the chilled dough down; turn out onto a lightly floured surface. Cover and let rest for 10 minutes.

Roll the dough to about ½-inch thickness. Cut with floured doughnut cutter. Cover and let rise in a warm place till *very light* (30 to 40 minutes). Meanwhile, prepare Eggnog Glaze and set aside.

On the *range top,* in a saucepan or deep-fat fryer heat cooking oil to 375°. Fry doughnuts, a few at a time, for 1½ to 2 minutes, turning once. Drain on paper toweling. While warm, dip the doughnut tops in the Eggnog Glaze. Makes about 24 doughnuts.

Eggnog Glaze: In a mixing bowl stir together 2 cups sifted *powdered sugar,* dash *ground nutmeg* and enough *dairy or canned eggnog* (about 3 tablespoons) to make of drizzling consistency.

ORANGE CREME CREPES

½ cup sugar
  3 tablespoons all-purpose flour
    Dash salt
1¼ cups orange juice
  1 teaspoon lemon juice
  1 beaten egg yolk
  1 tablespoon butter *or* margarine
16 Basic Dessert Crepes
  1 teaspoon vanilla
  1 cup whipping cream
    Powdered sugar *or* chocolate-flavored syrup (optional)

For filling, in a 4-cup glass measure combine sugar, flour, and salt. Stir in orange juice and lemon juice. In the *microwave oven* cook, uncovered, on high power for 4 to 6 minutes or till the mixture is thickened and bubbly, stirring twice during cooking.

Gradually add about *half* of the hot mixture to the beaten egg yolk, stirring constantly. Return all to the glass measure. Micro-cook, uncovered, on high about 30 seconds or till slightly thickened, stirring after every 10 seconds. Add butter or margarine to hot mixture, stirring till melted. Cover surface with clear plastic wrap; cool slightly.

On the *range top* prepare the Basic Dessert Crepes as directed in recipe at right, *except* add the vanilla to batter.

For filling, beat the whipping cream till soft peaks form. Fold whipped cream into the cooled orange mixture.

To assemble, spoon about ¼ *cup* of the filling along center of unbrowned side of one crepe. Fold the two opposite edges so they overlap atop filling. Repeat with remaining crepes and filling. Serve the crepes seam side down. Sprinkle with powdered sugar or drizzle with chocolate syrup, if desired. Makes 8 servings.

RASPBERRY CREPE CRISPS

  1 10-ounce package frozen red raspberries
12 to 14 Basic Dessert Crepes
    Cooking oil for deep-fat frying
    Powdered sugar
  2 tablespoons sugar
  1 tablespoon cornstarch
  1 tablespoon lemon juice
  2 tablespoons brandy

Thaw raspberries; sieve and discard seeds. Prepare Basic Dessert Crepes and stack in two stacks; cut into 1-inch strips. Cut strips in half. Separate the crepes into single layers. On the *range top,* fry crepe pieces, a few at a time, in deep hot oil (365°) about 1 minute or till brown. Drain on paper toweling in a single layer. Sprinkle with powdered sugar.

For dip, in a 2-cup glass measure combine sugar and cornstarch. Stir in lemon juice; add raspberries. In the *microwave oven* cook, uncovered, on high power about 2 minutes or till thickened and bubbly, stirring after every 30 seconds. Micro-cook, uncovered, on high for 1 minute more, stirring after 30 seconds. Stir in the brandy. Serve with the crepe crisps. Makes 8 to 10 servings.

BASIC DESSERT CREPES

1½ cups milk
  1 cup all-purpose flour
  2 eggs
  2 tablespoons sugar
  1 tablespoon cooking oil
  ⅛ teaspoon salt

Combine milk, flour, eggs, sugar, oil, and salt. Beat till smooth. On the *range top* heat a lightly greased 6-inch skillet. Remove from heat. Spoon in 2 tablespoons batter; lift and tilt skillet to spread. Return to heat; brown on one side. Invert pan to remove crepe. Repeat to make 16 to 18 crepes, greasing skillet occasionally.

Filling and Folding Prune and Walnut Dumplings

Place about ½ teaspoon of the nut mixture in the center of one circle of dough. Do not use too much walnut mixture or the dumplings will be hard to seal. Place a cooked prune atop the nut mixture. Moisten the edges of the circle with water. (This will help keep the edges of the dumpling sealed while it is cooking.) Gently fold sides of the circle around the filling, as shown. Repeat with the remaining dough, nut mixture, and prunes.

Using your fingers, gently pinch the edges of the dough together, as shown. You can also use the tines of a fork to close the dumplings. Make sure the filling is sealed inside the dough.

Cover the dumplings with a damp cloth to prevent them from drying out while folding and sealing remaining dumplings.

PRUNE AND WALNUT DUMPLINGS

- 18 pitted, dried prunes
- 1 cup water
- ½ cup chopped walnuts
- ¼ cup sugar
- 1 teaspoon ground cinnamon
- 1¼ cups all-purpose flour
- ¼ cup water
- 1 beaten egg
- ½ teaspoon salt
- Dairy sour cream (optional)

In a 1-quart nonmetal casserole combine prunes and the 1 cup water. In the *microwave oven* cook, covered, on high power for 3 to 4 minutes or till prunes are tender. Drain and set aside. Combine walnuts, sugar, and cinnamon; set aside.

For dough, in a mixing bowl stir together the flour, the ¼ cup water, beaten egg, and salt to make a moderately soft dough. If necessary, stir in 1 to 2 tablespoons additional *all-purpose flour*. Turn out onto a lightly floured surface. Knead gently for 3 to 5 strokes.

Roll or pat dough to ¼-inch thickness. With a floured 2½-inch biscuit cutter, cut the dough into 18 circles, dipping the cutter in *all-purpose flour* between cuts. Reroll dough as necessary. Place about ½ *teaspoon* of the nut mixture in the center of *one* dough circle; top with a prune. Lightly moisten edges of dough; bring dough up around the filling and pinch together to seal. Repeat with the remaining dough circles, nut mixture, and prunes. (Keep the uncooked filled dumplings covered with a damp towel to prevent drying.)

On the *range top*, cover and cook dumplings, half at a time, in a large amount of boiling water for 7 to 8 minutes. Remove with slotted spoon and drain on paper toweling.

If the dumplings cool before serving, cover and cook in the *microwave oven* on high power about 30 seconds or till heated through. To serve, place three dumplings on each serving plate; sprinkle with remaining nut mixture. Dollop with sour cream, if desired. Makes 6 servings.

PEANUT BUTTER-BROWN RICE PUDDING

This peanut butter lover's dessert finishes cooking as it stands—

⅓ **cup brown rice**
1 **slightly beaten egg**
¼ **cup peanut butter**
3 **tablespoons honey**
½ **teaspoon ground cinnamon**
1 **cup milk**
¼ **cup raisins *or* chopped pitted dates**
  Whipped cream *or* pressurized dessert topping (optional)
  Peanuts (optional)

On the *range top*, in a medium saucepan cook the brown rice according to package directions.

In a large mixing bowl combine the beaten egg, peanut butter, honey, cinnamon, and cooked brown rice. Add milk and raisins or chopped dates; stir till combined. Turn the mixture into a 1-quart nonmetal casserole.

Place a 9-inch nonmetal pie plate in the *microwave oven*. Place the filled casserole on the pie plate. Pour boiling water into the pie plate around the casserole to a depth of 1 inch. Micro-cook, covered, on high power for 4 minutes; stir the mixture thoroughly. Continue micro-cooking, covered, for 3 to 4 minutes or till the edges of the pudding are set and the center is creamy. Remove the casserole from water and let stand for 10 minutes.

Serve the pudding warm or chilled in dessert dishes. Top with whipped cream or pressurized dessert topping and peanuts, if desired. Makes 8 servings.

VEGETABLE TEMPURA WITH GARBANZO DIP

4 **cups desired vegetables (see options below)**
2 **tablespoons water**
1 **15-ounce can garbanzo beans, drained**
1 **8-ounce carton plain yogurt**
1 **clove garlic, minced**
¼ **teaspoon salt**
1 **cup all-purpose flour**
2 **tablespoons cornstarch**
½ **teaspoon salt**
1 **cup ice water**
1 **egg yolk**
1 **stiff-beaten egg white**
  Cooking oil for deep-fat frying

Place desired vegetables and the 2 tablespoons water in a 1½-quart non-metal casserole. In the *microwave oven* cook, covered, on high power about 5 minutes or till crisp-tender, stirring once.

Meanwhile, for dip, in a blender container or food processor bowl combine garbanzo beans, yogurt, garlic, and the ¼ teaspoon salt. Cover and blend or process till smooth. Set aside.

For batter, stir together flour, cornstarch, and the ½ teaspoon salt. Make a well in the center of the dry ingredients. Beat together the 1 cup ice water and egg yolk; add all at once to dry ingredients. Slowly stir just till moistened (the batter should be slightly lumpy). Fold in the stiff-beaten egg white. Place bowl of batter in larger bowl of ice water.

On the *range top* heat cooking oil to 375°. Dip desired vegetable pieces, one at a time, into batter, swirling to coat evenly. Fry the coated vegetables, a few pieces at a time, in hot oil for 4 to 5 minutes or till light brown. Drain on paper toweling. Keep warm while frying remaining vegetables. Arrange on a platter; serve with garbanzo dip. Makes 6 to 8 servings.

Vegetable Options: Choose from any combination of the following fresh or frozen vegetables: cut asparagus; broccoli buds; cauliflower flowerets; whole mushrooms; or peeled, sliced rutabagas, carrots, parsnips, or turnips.

ZUCCHINI-CHEESE EGG ROLLS

For smaller appetizer servings, cut these egg rolls into thirds—

1½ **cups coarsely chopped zucchini (1 medium)**
2 **tablespoons chopped onion**
1 **tablespoon butter *or* margarine**
¼ **teaspoon salt**
4 **egg roll skins**
1 **slice (1 ounce) American cheese, cut into 4 strips**
  Cooking oil *or* shortening for deep-fat frying

For filling, in a 1-quart nonmetal casserole combine chopped zucchini, onion, and butter or margarine. Cover and cook in the *microwave oven* on high power about 4 minutes or till tender, stirring once. Stir in the salt.

Place one egg roll skin with one point toward you. Spoon about *3 tablespoons* of the filling diagonally across and just below the center of the skin. Top with *1 strip* of the American cheese. Fold the bottom point of the egg roll skin over filling; tuck the point under the filling. Fold side corners of the skin over, forming an envelope shape. Roll up toward the remaining corner; moisten the point with a little water and press firmly to seal. Repeat with the remaining egg roll skins, zucchini filling, and cheese strips.

On the *range top*, in a large saucepan or deep-fat fryer heat cooking oil or shortening to 375°. Fry the egg rolls, two at a time, about 2 minutes or till golden brown. Makes 4 egg rolls.

MICROWAVE
PLUS OVEN

With your microwave and conventional ovens teaming up, you can feast on this deluxe Italian Pizza (see recipe, page 34). Just micro-cook the thick tomato sauce and spread it on the oven-crisped crust. Layer the mozzarella cheese, pepperoni, and tomato slices on top and bake the pizza conventionally.

The conventional oven does not cook foods as quickly as the microwave oven, though you can use that fact to your advantage. Its ability to cook slowly is essential to steam-leavened products that need time to rise during baking such as cream puffs, soufflés, and popovers.

The gradual baking process of the conventional oven also allows you more control over delicate foods, such as baked custards and other dishes that you would set in a pan of water to ensure even heat distribution during cooking.

It roasts large cuts of meat to a desirable brown tone. And when it boils down to golden piecrusts or breads, the conventional oven wins the blue ribbon. In addition to browning food, conventional baking will also add crispness to piecrusts and cookies by letting moisture evaporate from the surfaces. The microwave oven can produce a flaky piecrust too, but you must decide if the pale color is acceptable for each pastry recipe.

TARRAGON ROAST WITH BRUSSELS SPROUTS

- 1 **4-pound boneless beef top round roast**
- ¼ **teaspoon salt**
- ¼ **teaspoon dried tarragon, crushed**
  Dash pepper
- 4 **cups brussels sprouts**
- ¼ **cup water**
- ¼ **cup all-purpose flour**
- ¼ **cup water**
- 1 **tablespoon capers**
- 2 **teaspoons instant beef bouillon granules**
- ¼ **teaspoon dried tarragon, crushed**
  Dash pepper

Place meat, fat side up, on a rack in a shallow roasting pan. Stir together salt, ¼ teaspoon tarragon, and dash pepper; rub over the surface of the meat. Insert a meat thermometer into the meat. In the *conventional oven* roast, uncovered, at 325° about 2¼ hours or till the meat thermometer registers 150° for rare to 170° for well-done.

Meanwhile, halve any large brussels sprouts. Place brussels sprouts in a 1½-quart nonmetal casserole; add ¼ cup water. In the *microwave oven* cook, covered, on high power about 10 minutes or till brussels sprouts are tender. Transfer the meat to a serving platter, reserving pan juices. Arrange brussels sprouts around meat; keep warm.

For gravy, pour the reserved meat juices into a 4-cup glass measure. Skim off fat. Add enough water to juices to make 1¾ cups liquid. Stir together flour and ¼ cup water; stir into meat juices. Stir in capers, beef bouillon granules, ¼ teaspoon tarragon, and dash pepper. Micro-cook, uncovered, on high for 2 to 4 minutes or till thickened and bubbly, stirring after every 30 seconds. Micro-cook, uncovered, on high for 1 minute more, stirring once during cooking.

Spoon some of gravy over the roast and brussels sprouts. Pass the remaining gravy. Makes 8 to 10 servings.

MEAT LOAF EN CROUTE

- 2 **beaten eggs**
- ⅓ **cup chopped onion**
- ¼ **cup fine dry bread crumbs**
- 1 **clove garlic, minced**
- ½ **teaspoon dried oregano, crushed**
- ¼ **teaspoon fennel seed, crushed**
- 1½ **pounds ground beef**
- 1¾ **cups all-purpose flour**
- ¼ **cup grated Parmesan cheese**
- 1 **tablespoon snipped parsley**
- ⅔ **cup shortening *or* lard**
- 2 **tablespoons butter *or* margarine**
- 1 **8-ounce can pizza sauce**
- 2 **tablespoons burgundy**

Combine beaten eggs, onion, bread crumbs, garlic, oregano, fennel, ¼ teaspoon *salt*, and ⅛ teaspoon *pepper*. Add beef; mix well. Pat into an 8x4x2-inch nonmetal loaf dish. If desired, insert a microwave meat thermometer into center. In the *microwave oven* cook, uncovered, on high power about 5 minutes or till thermometer registers 130°, giving the dish a half-turn once. Drain off fat.

Stir together flour, Parmesan cheese, parsley, and ¼ teaspoon *salt*. Cut in shortening till pieces are the size of small peas. Add ⅓ to ½ cup cold *water, 1 tablespoon* at a time, tossing with a fork till all is moistened. Form into a ball. On a lightly floured surface roll pastry into a 12x10-inch rectangle.

Micro-cook butter or margarine, uncovered, on high for 40 to 60 seconds or till melted. Center meat atop pastry. Brush long sides of pastry with melted butter. Overlap atop meat, pinching to seal. Trim excess pastry from each end; brush ends with melted butter. Fold ends up and seal. Place, seam side down, on a greased baking sheet. Brush again with butter. In the *conventional oven* bake at 425° about 20 minutes or till golden.

Meanwhile, stir together pizza sauce and burgundy. In the *microwave oven* cook, covered, on high power about 2 minutes or till heated through. Serve with meat loaf. Makes 6 servings.

TAMALE PIE

- 1 pound ground beef
- ½ cup chopped onion
- ¼ cup chopped green pepper
- 1 clove garlic, minced
- 1 8¾-ounce can whole kernel corn, drained
- 1 8-ounce can tomato sauce
- ¼ cup sliced pimiento-stuffed olives
- 1½ teaspoons chili powder
- ¼ teaspoon dried oregano, crushed
- ⅛ teaspoon pepper
- 1¼ cups milk
- ⅓ cup cornmeal
- 1 tablespoon butter or margarine
- ¾ teaspoon salt
- 1 cup shredded cheddar or Monterey Jack cheese
- 2 slightly beaten eggs
  Green pepper rings (optional)

In a 10x6x2-inch nonmetal baking dish stir together ground beef, onion, chopped green pepper, and garlic. In the *microwave oven* cook the ground beef mixture, covered, on high power about 5 minutes or till meat is no longer pink and vegetables are tender, stirring once during cooking. Drain off fat. Stir in corn, tomato sauce, sliced olives, chili powder, oregano, and pepper. Micro-cook, uncovered, on high for 3 to 4 minutes or till mixture is heated through.

Meanwhile, in a medium saucepan stir together milk, cornmeal, butter or margarine, and salt. On the *range top* cook and stir till thickened and bubbly. Cook and stir for 1 minute more. Remove from heat. Stir about *two-thirds* of the shredded cheese into the thickened cornmeal mixture; stir in the eggs.

Spoon the cornmeal mixture atop the meat mixture in baking dish. In the *conventional oven* bake at 375° for 30 to 35 minutes. Sprinkle the remaining shredded cheese atop. Bake for 3 to 4 minutes more or till the cheese is melted. Garnish with green pepper rings, if desired. Makes 8 servings.

PARMESAN MEAT PUFF

- 1 9-ounce package frozen Italian green beans or one 9-ounce package frozen cut green beans
- 2 tablespoons water
- 1 pound ground beef or Italian sausage
- 2 tablespoons butter or margarine
- 2 tablespoons all-purpose flour
- 1 teaspoon chili powder
- ½ teaspoon salt
- 1 cup milk
- ½ cup shredded American cheese (2 ounces)
- 1 tablespoon chopped canned pimiento, drained
- 3 egg yolks
- 2 tablespoons grated Parmesan cheese
- 3 egg whites

In an 8x1½-inch round nonmetal baking dish combine green beans and the water. In the *microwave oven* cook, covered, on high power for 4 to 7 minutes or till tender. Drain; set aside. In a 1-quart nonmetal casserole micro-cook beef or sausage, covered, on high for 5 minutes, stirring twice. Drain off fat; set aside.

Micro-cook butter or margarine, uncovered, on high for 45 to 60 seconds or till melted. Stir in flour, chili powder, and salt. Add milk; micro-cook, covered, on high for 4 to 5 minutes or till thickened and bubbly, stirring after every minute. Add cheese; stir till melted. Stir in the ground beef or sausage and pimiento; set aside.

Beat egg yolks till thick and lemon colored. Stir in Parmesan cheese.

Micro-cook the meat mixture, uncovered, on high for 2 to 3 minutes or till heated through; spread atop beans.

Using clean beaters, beat egg whites till stiff peaks form (tips stand straight). Fold egg yolk mixture into egg whites; spread atop hot mixture in dish. In the *conventional oven* bake at 350° for 20 to 25 minutes or till golden. Serve immediately. Makes 6 servings.

BAVARIAN MEAT RING

Make soft rye bread crumbs for the meat loaf by tearing 2 slices of fresh rye bread into crumbs. Or, tear the two bread slices into quarters. Place bread, a few pieces at a time, in a blender container; cover and blend till coarsely chopped—

- 2 beaten eggs
- ¾ cup apple juice
- 1½ cups soft rye bread crumbs (2 slices)
- ½ cup finely chopped onion
- 1½ teaspoons salt
- 1 teaspoon dried sage, crushed
- 2 pounds ground beef, pork, or lamb
  Paprika
- 1 16-ounce can sauerkraut
- 2 medium carrots, shredded (¾ cup)
- ½ cup apple juice
- 2 tablespoons brown sugar
- 2 teaspoons caraway seed

In a mixing bowl stir together beaten eggs and the ¾ cup apple juice. Stir in rye bread crumbs, chopped onion, salt, and sage. Add the ground meat; mix well. Pat the meat mixture into a 5½- or 6-cup ring mold; unmold into a shallow baking pan. Sprinkle with paprika. In the *conventional oven* bake at 350° for 50 to 55 minutes or till done.

In a 2-quart nonmetal casserole stir together *undrained* sauerkraut, shredded carrot, the ½ cup apple juice, brown sugar, and caraway seed. In the *microwave oven* cook, covered, on high power about 8 minutes or till heated through, stirring once during cooking; drain.

Transfer the meat loaf to a serving platter. Spoon the hot sauerkraut mixture into the center of the meat loaf ring. Makes 8 servings.

CREOLE-STYLE PORK ROAST

¼ cup chopped onion
¼ cup chopped green pepper
1 tablespoon butter *or* margarine
2 teaspoons Creole Seasoning Mix
1 4-ounce can mushroom stems and pieces, drained
½ cup tomato paste
1 4- to 5-pound boneless pork loin roast
   Cooking oil (optional)
2 tablespoons all-purpose flour
¼ to ½ teaspoon Creole Seasoning Mix

Combine onion, green pepper, butter or margarine, and the 2 teaspoons Creole Seasoning Mix. In the *microwave oven* cook, uncovered, on high power for 1 to 2 minutes or till tender; drain. Stir in mushrooms and ¼ *cup* tomato paste.

Untie and unroll roast; spread mixture atop. Reroll with mixture inside; retie. Place roast on a rack in a shallow roasting pan. Insert a meat thermometer. In the *conventional oven* roast at 325° for 2½ to 3 hours or till the thermometer registers 170°. Transfer roast to a serving platter, reserving pan juices; keep warm.

For gravy, skim and reserve fat from pan juices. Add water to juices to make 1½ cups liquid; set aside. In a 4-cup glass measure place 2 tablespoons reserved fat (add cooking oil, if necessary). Stir in the remaining tomato paste, flour, the ¼ to ½ teaspoon Creole Seasoning Mix, and ¼ teaspoon *salt*. Stir in reserved pan juices. In the *microwave oven* cook, uncovered, on high power for 2 to 3 minutes or till thickened and bubbly, stirring twice. Micro-cook, uncovered, for 1 minute more, stirring once. Serve gravy with meat. Serves 12 to 15.

Creole Seasoning Mix: Combine 4 teaspoons *ground red pepper*, 1 tablespoon *salt*, 1 teaspoon *chili powder*, 1 teaspoon *paprika*, 1 teaspoon *ground coriander*, 1 teaspoon *pepper*, ¾ teaspoon *ground cloves*, and ½ teaspoon *garlic powder*. Store, covered, in a cool place. (Creole-Style Crab on page 70 also calls for Creole Seasoning Mix.)

PORK LOIN ROYALE

Prepare the melon sauce at the last minute using your microwave oven, while the pork roasts conventionally—

1 3- to 5-pound boneless pork loin roast
½ teaspoon salt
½ pound bulk pork sausage
1 12-ounce can (1½ cups) apricot nectar
4 teaspoons cornstarch
2 cups cubed cantaloupe, honeydew melon, *or* other melon (except watermelon)
1 tablespoon lemon juice
   Parsley sprigs (optional)
   Melon balls (optional)

Untie pork roast; unroll to lie flat. Sprinkle the inside surface of meat with salt. Spread the pork sausage atop. Reroll roast with sausage inside; retie securely with string. Place the stuffed roast on a rack in a shallow roasting pan. Insert a meat thermometer into meat. In the *conventional oven* roast the pork at 325° for 1¾ to 2¾ hours or till the meat thermometer registers 170°.

For sauce, in a 4-cup glass measure stir together apricot nectar and cornstarch. In the *microwave oven* cook, uncovered, on high power for 4 to 5 minutes or till thickened and bubbly, stirring after every minute. Stir in melon pieces and lemon juice. Micro-cook, uncovered, on high for 1 minute more or till the sauce is heated through.

Transfer the roast to a serving platter. Garnish with parsley and melon balls, if desired. Serve the melon sauce with meat. Makes 9 to 15 servings.

PORK AND FRUIT PIE

1 cup water
½ cup chopped mixed dried fruit
1 pound ground pork
¼ cup chopped onion
⅓ cup fine dry bread crumbs
½ teaspoon salt
⅛ teaspoon ground cinnamon
   Dash ground cloves
   Dash pepper
   Pastry for Double-Crust Pie

In the *microwave oven*, in a small nonmetal bowl cook water, uncovered, on high power for 2 to 4 minutes or till boiling. Add dried fruit. Let stand for 5 minutes. *Do not drain.*

In a 1-quart nonmetal casserole combine ground pork and onion. Microcook, uncovered, on high power about 5 minutes or till pork is no longer pink, stirring twice during cooking. Drain off fat. Stir in undrained fruit, bread crumbs, salt, cinnamon, cloves, and pepper.

Prepare Pastry for Double-Crust Pie. On a lightly floured surface flatten 1 ball of dough with hands. Roll dough from center to edge, forming a circle about 12 inches in diameter. Ease pastry into a 9-inch pie plate, being careful to avoid stretching pastry; trim pastry even with rim of pie plate. For top crust, roll out second ball of dough. Cut slits for escape of steam. Place meat mixture in pie shell. Top with pastry for top crust. Trim top crust ½ inch beyond edge of pie plate. Fold extra pastry under bottom crust; flute edge.

In the *conventional oven* bake pie at 400° about 30 minutes or till golden brown. If necessary, cover the edges of pastry with foil to prevent overbrowning. Makes 6 servings.

Pastry for Double-Crust Pie: In medium mixing bowl stir together 2 cups *all-purpose flour* and 1 teaspoon *salt*. Cut in ⅔ cup *shortening or lard* till pieces are the size of small peas. Sprinkle 1 tablespoon *water* over part of mixture; gently toss with a fork. Push to side of bowl. Repeat, using 5 to 6 tablespoons more *water,* till all is moistened. Form dough into 2 balls.

ITALIAN PIZZA

Pictured on page 30 and on the cover—

 5 **to 5½ cups all-purpose flour**
 1 **package active dry yeast**
 1 **cup grated Parmesan cheese**
 1½ **cups warm water (115° to 120°)**
 1 **egg**
 2 **tablespoons cooking oil**
    Cornmeal
    Tomato Sauce
 2 **cups shredded mozzarella**
    cheese
 6 **to 8 ounces sliced pepperoni**
 2 **medium tomatoes, sliced**
    Green pepper rings (optional)
 ⅓ **cup snipped parsley**

Combine *2 cups* of the flour, yeast, and *½ cup* of the Parmesan cheese. Stir in warm water, egg, and cooking oil. Beat on low speed of electric mixer for ½ minute, scraping bowl. Beat 3 minutes on high speed. Stir in as much remaining flour as you can mix in with a spoon. On a floured surface knead in enough remaining flour to make a moderately stiff dough (about 5 minutes total). Place dough in greased bowl; turn once. Cover; let rise in a warm place till double (about 1 hour). Punch down; divide in half. Cover; let rest 10 minutes. Sprinkle cornmeal on two greased 12-inch pizza pans. Pat or roll dough into pans, making a ½-inch rim. Cover; let rise about 15 minutes. In the *conventional oven* prebake the crusts at 375° for 20 to 25 minutes.

Prepare Tomato Sauce; spread on crusts. Top with mozzarella cheese, pepperoni, tomatoes, green pepper rings, if desired, and remaining Parmesan. In the *conventional oven* bake at 375° for 5 to 10 minutes more or till heated through. Top with parsley. Makes 2 pizzas.

Tomato Sauce: In the *microwave oven* cook ½ cup chopped *onion* in 2 tablespoons *cooking oil,* covered, on high power for 2 to 3 minutes or till tender. Stir in 1½ cups *water,* one 6-ounce can *tomato paste,* and 1½ teaspoons dried *basil,* crushed. Micro-cook, uncovered, on high for 5 minutes more, stirring once.

SPINACH-STUFFED HAM

 1 **pound fresh spinach, chopped**
    (6 cups)
 ½ **cup finely chopped cabbage**
 ½ **cup finely chopped celery**
 ¼ **cup finely chopped onion**
 1 **tablespoon cooking oil**
 ½ **teaspoon dried sage, crushed**
 ½ **teaspoon dried marjoram,**
    crushed
 ¼ **teaspoon dry mustard**
    Dash pepper
    Dash ground red pepper
 1 **4½- to 5-pound fully cooked**
    boneless ham

For stuffing, in a 2-quart nonmetal casserole combine the chopped spinach, cabbage, celery, onion, and cooking oil. In the *microwave oven* cook, covered, on high power for 8 to 10 minutes or till vegetables are crisp-tender, stirring once or twice during cooking. Drain well in a colander, squeezing out excess liquid. Return the spinach mixture to casserole; stir in sage, marjoram, dry mustard, pepper, and red pepper. Cool slightly.

Working lengthwise on ham, make a row of 2-inch-long slits, about 2 inches apart and 2½ to 3 inches deep. Make a second row of slits 1 inch away from first row, being sure the slits are not in line with the first ones. Repeat rows over top and sides of entire ham. Enlarge slits slightly by making a "V" in each one. Pack stuffing firmly into slits.

Place ham on a rack in a shallow baking pan. Insert a meat thermometer into the meat. Cover ham loosely with foil. In the *conventional oven* bake at 325° for 1¾ to 2 hours or till thermometer registers 140°. Makes 15 servings.

VEGETABLE-HAM ROLL WITH VEGETABLE SAUCE

Pictured on pages 4 and 5—

    Plain Pastry
 1 **8½-ounce can mixed vegetables**
 2 **tablespoons chopped onion**
 1 **tablespoon butter *or* margarine**
 1 **tablespoon all-purpose flour**
 ¼ **cup milk**
 1 **beaten egg**
 1 **6¾-ounce can chunk-style ham,**
    drained and flaked
    Vegetable Sauce

Prepare Plain Pastry; set aside. Drain vegetables, reserving liquid; set aside. In the *microwave oven* cook onion in butter or margarine, covered, on high power for 1 minute. Stir in flour and dash *pepper.* Add milk; micro-cook, uncovered, on high about 1 minute or till bubbly, stirring once. Reserve *1 tablespoon* of the egg. Stir ham, *half* of the vegetables, and milk mixture into remaining portion of egg.

Spread mixture in center of pastry. Fold sides and ends of pastry over, brushing edges with reserved egg. Pinch to seal. Place roll, seam side down, on a greased baking sheet. Brush with egg; cut slits. In the *conventional oven* bake at 400° for 40 to 45 minutes. Prepare Vegetable Sauce to serve with roll. Serves 4.

Plain Pastry: Stir together 1 cup *all-purpose flour* and ½ teaspoon *salt.* Cut in ⅓ cup *shortening or lard* till pieces are the size of small peas. Sprinkle 1 tablespoon *water* atop; toss. Repeat, using 2 to 3 tablespoons more *water,* till all is moistened. Form into a ball. On a floured surface roll into a 12x8-inch rectangle.

Vegetable Sauce: Add enough *milk* to reserved vegetable liquid to make ⅔ cup. In the *microwave oven* cook 1 tablespoon *butter or margarine,* uncovered, on high power for 30 seconds; stir in 1 tablespoon *all-purpose flour.* Add milk mixture; micro-cook, uncovered, on high for 3 minutes or till bubbly, stirring after every minute. Stir in reserved vegetables and ⅓ cup shredded *process Swiss cheese.* Micro-cook, uncovered, on high about 1 minute more or till cheese is melted.

TURKEY PUFF

- 1 9-ounce package frozen cut green beans
- 2 tablespoons water
- 1½ cups herb-seasoned stuffing mix *or* 2 cups leftover stuffing
- 1 10¾-ounce can condensed cream of mushroom soup
- ⅓ cup milk
- 1½ cups cubed cooked turkey
- 4 egg yolks
- 4 egg whites
- ½ cup canned French-fried onions (optional)

In a 1-quart nonmetal casserole combine frozen beans and the water. In a *microwave oven* cook, covered, on high power for 4 to 7 minutes, stirring once during cooking. Let stand, covered, for 3 minutes; drain.

Prepare stuffing mix according to package directions or use baked leftover stuffing. Pat the stuffing into a greased 12x7½x2-inch baking dish; set aside.

In a large nonmetal mixing bowl combine condensed cream of mushroom soup and milk. Stir in drained green beans and cubed turkey. Micro-cook the turkey mixture, covered, on high for 4 to 5 minutes or till heated through, stirring once during cooking.

Meanwhile, in a mixing bowl beat egg yolks on medium speed of an electric mixer about 5 minutes or till thick and lemon colored. Using clean beaters, beat egg whites till stiff peaks form (tips stand straight). Fold beaten egg yolks into stiff-beaten egg whites.

Carefully pour the hot turkey mixture over stuffing in baking dish; spread egg mixture atop turkey mixture. In the *conventional oven* bake, uncovered, at 350° for 25 minutes. Sprinkle with canned French-fried onions, if desired. Bake at 350° about 5 minutes more or till egg mixture is set. Makes 6 servings.

HARVEST STUFFED HEN

- ½ cup shredded carrot
- ½ cup chopped celery
- ½ medium onion, chopped (¼ cup)
- ¼ cup butter *or* margarine
- ½ teaspoon ground sage
- ¼ teaspoon salt
- ⅛ teaspoon ground cinnamon
  Dash pepper
- 4 cups dry whole wheat *or* white bread cubes
- 2 medium apples, peeled and finely chopped (1 cup)
- ¼ cup chopped walnuts
- 2 tablespoons toasted wheat germ
- ¼ to ⅓ cup chicken broth
- 1 5-pound whole roasting chicken
  Cooking oil

For stuffing, in the *microwave oven*, in a 1-quart nonmetal casserole cook carrot, celery, and onion in butter or margarine, covered, on high power about 3 minutes or till tender. Stir in sage, salt, cinnamon, and pepper. In a mixing bowl combine bread cubes, apple, walnuts, and wheat germ. Stir vegetable mixture into bread mixture. Drizzle with enough chicken broth to moisten; toss lightly.

Rinse chicken and pat dry with paper toweling. Rub inside of cavities with salt. Spoon some of the stuffing loosely into neck cavity; pull neck skin to back and fasten with a small skewer. Lightly spoon some of the stuffing into body cavity. Tie legs to tail. Twist wing tips under back. Place the remaining stuffing in the 1-quart nonmetal casserole; set aside.

Place chicken, breast side up, on a rack in a shallow roasting pan. Brush skin with cooking oil. Insert a meat thermometer. In the *conventional oven* roast, uncovered, at 375° for 2¼ to 2½ hours or till thermometer registers 185° and drumstick moves easily in socket. Brush dry areas occasionally with pan drippings.

Before serving, in the *microwave oven* cook remaining stuffing, covered, on high power about 2 minutes or till heated through. Makes 8 servings.

CHEESE-STUFFED CHICKEN ROLLS

- ⅓ cup chopped green pepper
- 2 tablespoons sliced green onion
- 1 tablespoon butter *or* margarine
- 1 beaten egg
- 1 cup shredded mozzarella cheese
- ½ cup ricotta cheese *or* dry cottage cheese, sieved
- 3 whole medium chicken breasts, skinned, halved lengthwise, and boned
- 6 frozen patty shells, thawed
  Milk
- 1 8-ounce can tomato sauce
- ¼ cup dry white wine
- ½ teaspoon sugar

In a 1-cup glass measure combine green pepper, green onion, and butter or margarine. In the *microwave oven* cook, covered, on high power about 2 minutes or till tender. Stir together beaten egg, mozzarella cheese, and ricotta or sieved cottage cheese. Stir green onion mixture into cheese mixture.

Place each chicken breast half between 2 pieces of clear plastic wrap. Pound out with a meat mallet to a ⅛-inch thickness, working from center to edges. Remove plastic wrap. Sprinkle with salt and pepper. Spoon about *3 tablespoons* of the cheese mixture in the center of each. Fold in sides; roll up jelly-roll style.

Roll out each patty shell into an 8x6-inch rectangle. Place a chicken roll on each patty shell. Fold two opposite sides of patty shell atop chicken roll; moisten and seal sides. Fold ends atop chicken roll; moisten and seal. Place, seam side down, in a 15x10x1-inch baking pan. Brush milk atop rolls.

In the *conventional oven* bake at 350° about 50 minutes or till done. If necessary, cover with foil after 40 minutes to prevent overbrowning.

Meanwhile, for sauce, in a 2-cup glass measure stir together tomato sauce, dry white wine, and sugar. In the *microwave oven* cook, uncovered, on high power for 1 to 2 minutes or till heated through. Spoon sauce over chicken rolls. Makes 6 servings.

SEASIDE BUNDLES

    1 pound frozen fish fillets
    ¾ cup sliced green onion
    2 tablespoons butter or
        margarine
    1 beaten egg
    ½ cup water chestnuts, drained
        and chopped
    ½ cup shredded American cheese
        (2 ounces)
    ⅓ cup dairy sour cream
    ¼ cup fine dry bread crumbs
    1 2-ounce jar sliced pimiento,
        drained and chopped
    ¼ teaspoon pepper
    2 packages (8 each) refrigerated
        crescent rolls
        Shredded American cheese or
        dairy sour cream

Unwrap frozen fish and place in a 10x6x2-inch nonmetal baking dish. Cover with vented clear plastic wrap. In the *microwave oven* cook on high power for 8 to 10 minutes or till fish flakes easily when tested with a fork, giving dish a half-turn once during cooking. Drain well and flake. Set aside.

For filling, in a 1-quart nonmetal casserole micro-cook green onion in butter or margarine, covered, on high about 3 minutes or till tender. Stir in egg, chopped water chestnuts, the ½ cup shredded cheese, the ⅓ cup dairy sour cream, bread crumbs, pimiento, and pepper. Stir in flaked fish.

Unroll the crescent roll dough. Separate into 8 rectangles, using two rolls for each rectangle. Seal perforations.

Spoon a generous ⅓ cup filling onto each rectangle. Fold dough over filling; seal with tines of a fork. Place on an ungreased baking sheet. In the *conventional oven* bake at 425° about 10 minutes or till golden brown. To serve, top each bundle with additional shredded cheese or dairy sour cream. Makes 8 servings.

SAFFRON SHRIMP

You should always bake frozen patty shells conventionally to achieve a light, flaky texture—

    12 ounces fresh or frozen shelled
        shrimp (1 pound unshelled)
    4 frozen patty shells
    2 tablespoons chopped green
        onion
    2 tablespoons chopped celery
    2 tablespoons butter or margarine
    2 tablespoons all-purpose flour
    2 teaspoons Dijon-style mustard
    ¼ teaspoon crushed thread
        saffron or ground turmeric
    ⅛ teaspoon salt
        Dash pepper
    ¼ cup chicken broth
    ¼ cup light cream or milk
    ¼ cup dry white wine
        Snipped parsley (optional)

Thaw shrimp, if frozen. In the *conventional oven* bake the patty shells according to package directions.

Meanwhile, in a 1-quart nonmetal casserole combine shrimp, green onion, celery, and butter or margarine. In the *microwave oven* cook, covered, on high power about 4½ minutes or till shrimp are opaque, stirring twice during cooking. Stir in flour, Dijon-style mustard, saffron or turmeric, salt, and pepper. Add chicken broth and light cream or milk all at once. Micro-cook, uncovered, on high about 4 minutes or till thickened and bubbly, stirring twice during cooking. Stir in the white wine. Micro-cook, uncovered, on high for 30 seconds more or till heated through. Serve the shrimp mixture in the baked patty shells. Sprinkle with snipped parsley, if desired. Makes 4 servings.

APPLE-CHEDDAR QUICHE

    ¼ cup butter or margarine
    1 tablespoon finely chopped
        onion
    1¼ cups crushed stone-ground
        whole wheat crackers
    ¼ cup finely chopped walnuts
    2 large tart apples, peeled, cored,
        and sliced (2 cups)
    3 eggs
    1 cup cream-style cottage
        cheese
    1 cup shredded cheddar cheese
        (4 ounces)
    ¼ cup milk
    ½ teaspoon salt
        Dash pepper
        Ground nutmeg
        Shredded cheddar cheese
        (optional)

In a 4-cup glass measure combine butter or margarine and onion. In the *microwave oven* cook, covered, on high power for 1 to 2 minutes or till onion is tender. Stir in crushed crackers and walnuts. Press mixture into a 9-inch nonmetal pie plate, forming a crust. Micro-cook, uncovered, on high power for 2 to 3 minutes or till set, giving dish a half-turn once or twice during cooking.

In a nonmetal mixing bowl micro-cook apple slices in a small amount of water, covered, on high power for 2 to 3 minutes or till tender; drain. Arrange apple slices in the crust.

For filling, in a blender container or food processor bowl combine eggs, cottage cheese, the 1 cup cheddar cheese, milk, salt, and pepper. Cover and blend till the mixture is nearly smooth. Pour into crust. Sprinkle nutmeg atop.

In the *conventional oven* bake at 325° about 45 minutes or till a knife inserted near the center comes out clean. Sprinkle with additional cheddar cheese, if desired. Let stand for 10 minutes. Makes 5 servings.

Apple-Cheddar Quiche

EASY SELF-SAUCED SOUFFLÉ

The cheese topping puffs during baking, like a soufflé—

- 2 cups fresh peas *or* one 10-ounce package frozen peas
- ½ cup chicken broth
- ½ cup light cream *or* milk
- 2 tablespoons cornstarch
- 1 teaspoon snipped fresh dillweed *or* ¼ teaspoon dried dillweed
- ¼ teaspoon salt
  Dash pepper
- 4 eggs
- ¼ cup light cream *or* milk
- ½ teaspoon prepared mustard
- ⅛ teaspoon pepper
- 2 3-ounce packages cream cheese, cubed
- 1¼ cups cubed Swiss cheese (5 ounces)
  Fresh dill

In a 1½-quart nonmetal casserole combine fresh or frozen peas and chicken broth. In the *microwave oven* cook, covered, on high power for 4 to 6 minutes or till just tender, stirring once during cooking; *do not* drain. Stir together the ½ cup light cream or milk and cornstarch; add to pea mixture. Stir in snipped fresh or dried dillweed, salt, and the dash pepper. Micro-cook, uncovered, on high for 4 to 6 minutes or till thickened and bubbly, stirring after every minute.

In a blender container combine eggs, the ¼ cup cream or milk, mustard, and the ⅛ teaspoon pepper; cover and blend till smooth. With blender running, add cream cheese cubes and Swiss cheese cubes through the opening in the lid, blending till the mixture is smooth.

Carefully pour the cheese mixture over pea mixture in casserole. In the *conventional oven* bake at 375° for 40 to 45 minutes or till eggs are puffed and set. Garnish with fresh dillweed, if desired. Makes 6 servings.

CRUSTY HAM SOUFFLÉ

- 2 tablespoons butter *or* margarine
- ¼ cup finely shredded cheddar cheese (1 ounce)
- ¼ cup fine dry bread crumbs
- ¼ cup toasted wheat germ
- 1 cup sliced fresh mushrooms
- 3 tablespoons butter *or* margarine
- 3 tablespoons all-purpose flour
- 1 cup milk
- ½ cup finely shredded cheddar cheese (2 ounces)
- 4 egg yolks
- 1 cup diced fully cooked ham
- 4 egg whites

For crust, in the *microwave oven* cook the 2 tablespoons butter or margarine in a 1½-quart nonmetal soufflé dish, uncovered, on high power for 30 to 40 seconds or till melted. Stir in the ¼ cup shredded cheddar cheese, fine dry bread crumbs, and toasted wheat germ. Press the crumb mixture up sides of soufflé dish.

In a nonmetal bowl or a 4-cup glass measure combine sliced mushrooms and the 3 tablespoons butter or margarine; micro-cook, covered, on high for 2 to 3 minutes or till tender. Stir flour into mushroom mixture. Add milk all at once; mix well. Micro-cook, uncovered, on high for 4 to 5 minutes or till mixture is thickened and bubbly, stirring after every minute. Add the ½ cup shredded cheddar cheese, stirring till melted.

In a mixing bowl beat egg yolks for 5 minutes or till thick and lemon colored. Gradually stir the cheese mixture into egg yolks. Fold in ham. Using clean beaters, beat egg whites till stiff peaks form (tips stand straight).

Fold the cheese mixture into egg whites. Turn the mixture into the prepared soufflé dish. In the *conventional oven* bake at 325° for 55 to 60 minutes or till puffed and set. Serve immediately. Makes 4 to 6 servings.

ASPARAGUS AND EGG PUFF

- ½ cup butter *or* margarine
- 1 cup water
- 1 cup all-purpose flour
- ¼ teaspoon salt
- 4 eggs
- 1 cup frozen cut asparagus *or* frozen cut green beans
- ½ cup sliced fresh mushrooms
- 2 tablespoons finely chopped onion
- 2 tablespoons water
- 8 eggs
- ¼ cup dairy sour cream
- ¼ cup milk
- ¼ teaspoon dried thyme, crushed
- ¼ teaspoon pepper
- 1 cup shredded Swiss *or* cheddar cheese

For puff, on the *range top* melt the butter or margarine in a saucepan. Add the 1 cup water; bring to boiling. Add flour and salt all at once; stir vigorously. Cook and stir till mixture forms a ball that doesn't separate. Remove from heat; cool slightly, about 5 minutes.

Add the 4 eggs, one at a time, beating with a wooden spoon after each addition for 1 to 2 minutes or till smooth. Spread dough over bottom and up sides of a greased 9-inch pie plate. In the *conventional oven* bake at 400° for 30 to 35 minutes or till golden brown and puffed.

Meanwhile, in an 8x1½-inch round nonmetal baking dish combine frozen asparagus or green beans, sliced mushrooms, chopped onion, and the 2 tablespoons water. In the *microwave oven* cook, covered, on high power for 5 to 7 minutes or till tender, stirring once; drain.

In a mixing bowl combine the 8 eggs, sour cream, milk, thyme, and pepper; pour over vegetables. Micro-cook, uncovered, on high for 4 to 6 minutes or till eggs are almost set, pushing cooked portions to center of dish several times. Sprinkle with cheese. Micro-cook, uncovered, on high for 1 minute more or till cheese is melted. Spoon egg mixture into the baked puff. Cut into wedges to serve. Serve immediately. Makes 6 servings.

BROCCOLI STRATA

1 **10-ounce package frozen chopped broccoli**
2 **tablespoons water**
4 **slices whole wheat bread**
4 **slices American cheese (4 ounces)**
1 **2-ounce jar pimiento, drained and chopped (¼ cup)**
4 **slices process Swiss cheese (4 ounces)**
4 **eggs**
2 **cups milk**
¼ **cup finely chopped onion**
½ **teaspoon prepared mustard Dash pepper**
2 **slices whole wheat bread**
2 **tablespoons butter *or* margarine**

In a 1-quart nonmetal casserole combine frozen broccoli and the water. In the *microwave oven* cook, covered, on high power for 4 to 5 minutes or till tender, stirring once during cooking. Drain well.

Arrange the 4 slices of whole wheat bread in an ungreased 9x9x2-inch baking pan. Top with American cheese slices, then the broccoli and chopped pimiento. Place the Swiss cheese slices atop.

In a mixing bowl beat the eggs; stir in milk, chopped onion, prepared mustard, and pepper. Pour over the layers in the baking pan. Cover and chill in the *refrigerator* at least 1 hour.

Meanwhile, for topping, tear up the 2 slices of whole wheat bread; place in a blender container. Cover and blend at low speed till crumbs form. In the *microwave oven* cook the butter or margarine, uncovered, on high power for 40 to 50 seconds or till melted. Stir in bread crumbs. Cover and chill.

Sprinkle the bread crumb topping over the egg mixture. In the *conventional oven* bake, uncovered, at 325° for 60 to 65 minutes or till a knife inserted near the center comes out clean. Let stand 10 minutes. Makes 6 servings.

SAUSAGE IN PHYLLO

1 **10-ounce package frozen cut broccoli**
1 **cup sliced fresh mushrooms**
¾ **pound Italian sausage**
2 **8-ounce packages cream cheese**
1 **egg**
2 **cups shredded Monterey Jack cheese**
¼ **teaspoon garlic powder**
½ **cup butter *or* margarine**
9 **17x13-inch sheets phyllo dough**
1 **beaten egg**

In a 2-quart nonmetal casserole combine broccoli and 2 tablespoons *water*. In the *microwave oven* cook, covered, on high power about 3 minutes or till nearly done, stirring once. Add mushrooms; micro-cook, covered, on high for 2 minutes more or till tender. Let stand 3 minutes.

In a 1-quart nonmetal casserole micro-cook sausage, loosely covered, on high for 3 to 5 minutes or till no longer pink, stirring twice; drain off fat.

Meanwhile, in a mixing bowl beat cream cheese on medium speed of electric mixer for 30 seconds. Add 1 egg; beat till fluffy. Stir in shredded Monterey Jack cheese and garlic powder.

In a nonmetal bowl micro-cook butter or margarine, uncovered, on high for 1¼ to 2 minutes or till melted. Brush the bottom of a 12x7½x2-inch baking dish with some melted butter. Place 1 sheet of phyllo in dish, allowing sides to overlap edges. Brush with more melted butter. Repeat with phyllo and butter 5 times.

Spread cheese mixture over phyllo; spread the broccoli-mushroom mixture over cheese, then top with Italian sausage. Fold edges of phyllo over filling. Cut remaining sheets of phyllo in half crosswise; place on top of mixture in dish, brushing each sheet with butter. With a sharp knife, score top layers of phyllo in a diamond pattern. In the *conventional oven* bake at 375° for 20 minutes. Brush with the 1 beaten egg; bake 5 to 10 minutes more or till golden. Let stand for 10 minutes before serving. Use a sharp knife to cut into squares. Makes 9 servings.

POTATO-CHEESE SOUP EN CROUTE

⅔ **cup butter *or* margarine**
1 **cup all-purpose flour**
⅓ **cup dairy sour cream**
¼ **teaspoon dried dillweed**
½ **cup sliced green onion**
½ **cup bias-sliced celery**
2 **tablespoons butter *or* margarine**
2 **cups chopped peeled potato**
1½ **cups chicken broth**
½ **teaspoon dry mustard**
1½ **cups milk**
3 **tablespoons all-purpose flour**
1½ **cups shredded cheddar cheese**
½ **cup beer**

Using a pastry blender, cut the ⅔ cup butter into the 1 cup flour till the pieces are the size of small peas. Stir in the sour cream and dillweed. Cover; chill in the *refrigerator* for at least 3 hours.

On a well-floured surface, roll chilled dough into an ⅛-inch-thick circle. Using a 3½-inch round biscuit cutter, cut dough into 8 rounds, rerolling as necessary. Place on an ungreased baking sheet. Cut out centers of 4 dough rounds with a 3¼- or 3-inch round cutter to form rings. Place pastry rings atop pastry rounds on the baking sheet. In the *conventional oven* bake pastry at 350° about 20 minutes or till golden brown. (If desired, bake the pastry centers to use as snacks later.)

Meanwhile, combine green onion, celery, and the 2 tablespoons butter. In the *microwave oven* cook, covered, on high power for 4 minutes. Add potato, chicken broth, and dry mustard. Micro-cook, covered, on high about 6 minutes or till vegetables are tender.

Combine the milk and the 3 tablespoons flour; stir into vegetable mixture. Micro-cook, uncovered, on high about 6 minutes or till thickened and bubbly, stirring after every minute. Add shredded cheddar cheese, stirring till melted. Add beer; micro-cook, uncovered, on high about 2 minutes or till heated through. Ladle into 4 soup bowls. Place one hot pastry circle atop each serving. Serve immediately. Makes 4 servings.

Filling and Serving Mexican Corn Popover Bake

Create an edible serving bowl for the corn mixture by preparing a giant popover. Because popovers are raised by steam and need a high temperature to set the crust after they rise, they can be baked only in the conventional oven. While the popover is baking, prepare the corn mixture in your microwave oven. Use a spoon to spread it evenly atop the hot popover, as shown.

Be sure to reduce the conventional oven temperature to 350° before baking the filled popover. Sprinkle the top with shredded cheddar cheese and then bake in a conventional oven till the popover is heated through, and the cheese is melted. Before serving, cut into wedges using a sharp knife, as shown. Then use a pie server to transfer the wedges to dinner plates.

MEXICAN CORN POPOVER BAKE

- 2 tablespoons butter *or* margarine
- 2 eggs
- ¾ cup all-purpose flour
- ¾ cup milk
- 1 tablespoon cooking oil
- ½ cup chopped onion
- 1 clove garlic, minced
- 1 tablespoon cooking oil
- 1 teaspoon dried oregano, crushed
- ½ to 1 teaspoon chili powder
- ¼ teaspoon ground cumin
- 1 17-ounce can whole kernel corn, drained
- 1 4-ounce can green chili peppers, rinsed, seeded, and chopped
- 1 4-ounce can sliced mushrooms, drained
- ¾ teaspoon seasoned salt
- ½ teaspoon sugar
- ½ cup shredded cheddar cheese

For popover, in the *microwave oven* cook butter or margarine in a 9-inch non-metal pie plate, uncovered, on high power for 30 to 40 seconds or till melted; swirl to coat bottom and sides. Place eggs, flour, milk, 1 tablespoon oil, and ¼ teaspoon *salt* in a blender container. Cover and blend for 30 seconds or till smooth. Pour into pie plate. In the *conventional oven* bake at 450° about 20 minutes or till puffed and golden brown. Reduce oven temperature to 350°.

In a 4-cup glass measure combine onion, garlic, 1 tablespoon cooking oil, oregano, chili powder, and cumin. In the *microwave oven* cook, covered, on high power about 2 minutes or till onion is tender. Stir in corn, chili peppers, mushrooms, seasoned salt, and sugar; microcook, covered, on high for 2 to 3 minutes or till heated through. Spoon corn mixture evenly over popover to within 1 inch of edge. Sprinkle with shredded cheese.

In the *conventional oven* bake at 350° for 15 to 20 minutes more or till cheese is melted. Cut into wedges. Serve immediately. Makes 8 servings.

ZUCCHINI, CARROT, AND BARLEY BAKE

Cook the zucchini, carrot, and barley in your microwave oven to speed up the cooking time, then stir the casserole together and finish baking it in the conventional oven—

- 2 **cups shredded zucchini**
- 1 **cup shredded carrot**
- ⅔ **cup water**
- ⅓ **cup quick-cooking barley**
- ½ **teaspoon salt**
- 2 **beaten eggs**
- 1 **cup milk**
- ½ **teaspoon dried basil, crushed**
  Dash pepper
- ½ **cup shredded Swiss cheese**
  (2 ounces)

In a 1-quart nonmetal casserole stir together shredded zucchini, carrot, water, quick-cooking barley, and salt. In the *microwave oven* cook the zucchini-carrot mixture, covered, on high power about 12 minutes or till the vegetables and barley are tender, stirring once or twice during cooking; drain.

In a mixing bowl stir together beaten eggs, milk, basil, and pepper; stir in the drained zucchini-carrot mixture. Turn the egg-vegetable mixture into an ungreased 8x1½-inch round baking dish.

In the *conventional oven* bake, uncovered, at 350° about 25 minutes or just till mixture is set. Sprinkle the top with shredded Swiss cheese. Return to the *conventional oven* and bake the casserole about 2 minutes more or till the cheese is melted. Makes 6 servings.

SOURDOUGH PUMPERNICKEL BREAD

- ¾ **cup Sourdough Starter**
- 2½ **to 3 cups all-purpose flour**
- ⅓ **cup bran cereal**
- ¼ **cup cornmeal**
- 1 **package active dry yeast**
- 2 **teaspoons caraway seed**
- ¼ **cup light molasses**
- 1 **square (1 ounce) semisweet chocolate**
- 1 **tablespoon butter *or* margarine**
- 1 **teaspoon instant coffee crystals**
- ½ **cup mashed cooked potatoes**
- 1 **cup rye flour**

Prepare Sourdough Starter. Mix *1½ cups* all-purpose flour, cereal, cornmeal, yeast, and caraway. Mix molasses, chocolate, butter, coffee, ¾ cup *water,* and 2 teaspoons *salt;* in the *microwave oven* cook, uncovered, on high power about 2 minutes or till chocolate is melted. Cool to lukewarm (115° to 120°). Stir into dry ingredients; stir in starter and potatoes. Beat on low speed of electic mixer ½ minute. Beat 3 minutes on high speed. Stir in rye flour and as much all-purpose flour as possible. Knead in enough remaining all-purpose flour to make a moderately soft dough (3 to 5 minutes total). Cover; let rise in warm place till double (about 1½ hours). (*Or,* let rise in the *microwave oven* about 8 minutes, following tip at right.) Punch down. Cover; let rest 10 minutes. Shape into a loaf. Place in a greased 9x5x3-inch nonmetal loaf dish. Cover; let rise till double (about 1 hour). (*Or,* let rise in *microwave oven* about 5 minutes.) In *conventional oven* bake at 375° for 35 to 40 minutes. Makes 1 loaf.

Sourdough Starter: Soften 1 package *active dry yeast* in ½ cup warm *water* (110° to 115°). Stir in 2 cups warm *water,* then 2 cups *all-purpose flour* and 1 tablespoon *sugar.* Beat till smooth. Cover with cheesecloth; let stand at room temperature 5 to 10 days; stir 3 times a day. After using some of the starter, add ¾ cup *water,* ¾ cup *all-purpose flour,* and 1 teaspoon *sugar.* Let stand till bubbly; chill. If not used, add 1 teaspoon *sugar* every 10 days.

RAISING YEAST BREADS

You may be able to shorten the time it takes to raise yeast breads by using your variable-power microwave oven. To test your microwave oven to see if you can use it for raising yeast breads, place 2 tablespoons of cold stick margarine in a custard cup in the center of the microwave oven cavity. Set the microwave oven to the 10% power (LOW) setting. Micro-cook margarine, uncovered, on 10% power (LOW) for 4 minutes. If the margarine is NOT completely melted at the end of this 4 minutes, you can satisfactorily raise bread in your microwave oven.

For microwave rising, measure 3 cups water into a 4-cup glass measure. Micro-cook the 3 cups water on high power for 6 to 8 minutes or till it is boiling. Set the water to the side in the microwave oven. Place the yeast bread dough in a greased nonmetal bowl. Place the bowl of dough beside the water in the microwave oven; cover loosely with waxed paper. Micro-cook on 10% power (LOW) till the dough has doubled in size.

If your microwave oven completely melts the 2 tablespoons stick margarine in less than 4 minutes, you'll have to allow your breads to rise conventionally.

For conventional rising, place the yeast bread dough in a greased bowl. Turn the dough over once to grease the entire surface of the dough. This helps keep it from drying out. Cover the bowl of dough with a cloth. Set the bowl in a warm draft-free place and let the dough rise till it has doubled.

Preparing Dough and Topping for Sweet Rolls

Test your microwave oven (see tip, page 41) to see if you can speed the time needed for the first rising of Sticky Maple Sweet Rolls with Bacon. If you can use your microwave oven, simply place the dough in a lightly greased nonmetal bowl and cover with waxed paper. Then follow the directions for microwave rising in the tip on page 41.

Micro-cook the maple-flavored sticky topping, then divide the mixture evenly among twenty-four 2½-inch muffin cups, as shown. You may want to stir the topping several times while spooning it into the muffin cups to prevent layers from forming. When you turn the rolls out after baking, the topping will be on top.

Instead of using a knife (which is apt to squash the rolls) to cut the roll of dough into slices, use a piece of ordinary sewing-weight or heavy-duty thread. Place the thread under the dough where you want to make the cut and pull it up around the sides. Crisscross the thread across the roll, pulling quickly as though tying a knot, as shown.

STICKY MAPLE SWEET ROLLS WITH BACON

3¾ **to 4¼ cups all-purpose flour**
  1 **package active dry yeast**
1¼ **cups milk**
  ½ **cup butter** *or* **margarine**
  ¼ **cup sugar**
  1 **egg**
  ¾ **cup butter** *or* **margarine**
  ⅔ **cup packed brown sugar**
  ¼ **teaspoon maple flavoring**
  6 **slices bacon**

In a mixer bowl combine *1½ cups* flour and yeast. In a 4-cup glass measure mix milk, the ½ cup butter, sugar, and 1 teaspoon *salt.* In the *microwave oven* cook milk mixture, uncovered, on high power for 4 minutes or just till warm (115° to 120°), stirring after every minute. Add to dry ingredients; add egg. Beat on low speed of electric mixer for ½ minute, scraping bowl. Beat 3 minutes on high speed. Stir in as much remaining flour as you can mix in with a spoon. Knead on a lightly floured surface to make a moderately soft dough that is smooth and elastic (3 to 5 minutes total). Place in greased bowl; turn once. Cover; let rise in a warm place till double (about 1½ hours). (*Or,* let rise in the *microwave oven* about 17 minutes, following tip on page 41.)

Meanwhile, in the *microwave oven* cook the ¾ cup butter or margarine, uncovered, on high power about 1 minute or till melted. Stir in brown sugar and maple flavoring. Distribute evenly among twenty-four 2½-inch muffin cups.

Place bacon between paper toweling on paper plate. Micro-cook on high for 5 to 6 minutes or till done; crumble and set aside. Punch dough down; divide in half. Cover; let rest 10 minutes. On a floured surface, roll each half into a 12x8-inch rectangle. Sprinkle with bacon. Roll up jelly-roll style, beginning with long side. Cut into 1-inch slices. Place, cut side down, in muffin cups. Cover; let rise in a warm place till double (25 to 30 minutes). (Do *not* let rise in *microwave oven.*) In the *conventional oven* bake at 350° for 25 to 30 minutes. Cool 2 to 3 minutes in pans. Invert onto wire rack. Makes 24 rolls.

BANANA-WALNUT CAKE

1¾ cups all-purpose flour
1 teaspoon baking soda
1 teaspoon baking powder
½ teaspoon salt
1½ cups sugar
¾ cup shortening
2 eggs
¾ cup mashed ripe banana
1 teaspoon vanilla
⅔ cup buttermilk *or* sour milk
½ cup chopped walnuts *or* pecans
Creamy Nut Filling
Frosting

Grease and flour two 9x1½-inch round baking pans. Stir together flour, baking soda, baking powder, and salt. Beat sugar and shortening with electric mixer till well combined. Add eggs, one at a time, beating for 1 minute after each. Add mashed banana and vanilla; beat 2 minutes more. Add the dry ingredients and buttermilk or sour milk alternately to beaten mixture, beating on low speed after each additon till just combined. Stir in nuts. Turn into prepared pans. In the *conventional oven* bake at 375° for 25 to 30 minutes or till done. Cool 10 minutes on wire racks. Remove from pans; cool.

Meanwhile, prepare Creamy Nut Filling; chill in the *refrigerator* for 1 to 2 hours. Place one cake layer on a serving plate. Spread Creamy Nut Filling atop; top with second layer. Prepare Frosting; frost top and sides. Makes 1 cake.

Creamy Nut Filling: Stir together ½ cup packed *brown sugar* and 2 tablespoons *all-purpose flour*; stir in ½ cup *evaporated milk* and 2 tablespoons *butter or margarine*. In the *microwave oven* cook, covered, on high power about 2 minutes or till thickened and bubbly, stirring after every 30 seconds. Stir in ⅓ cup finely chopped *walnuts or pecans*, ½ teaspoon *vanilla*, and dash *salt*.

Frosting: Beat 1 *egg white*, ½ cup *shortening*, ¼ cup *butter or margarine*, and 1 teaspoon *vanilla* on medium speed of electric mixer till well combined. Gradually add 2 cups sifted *powdered sugar*, beating till light and fluffy.

PRUNE-SPICE CAKE

8 ounces pitted dried prunes (1½ cups)
Water
2 cups all-purpose flour
1½ cups sugar
1¼ teaspoons baking soda
1 teaspoon salt
1 teaspoon ground cinnamon
1 teaspoon ground nutmeg
½ teaspoon ground cloves
½ cup cooking oil
3 eggs
2 tablespoons butter *or* margarine
½ cup sugar
2 tablespoons all-purpose flour
½ cup chopped walnuts

Cover prunes with water. In the *microwave oven* cook prunes, covered, on high power for 5 minutes. Let stand 5 minutes. Drain prunes, reserving ⅔ cup of the liquid. Chop prunes; set aside.

Grease and lightly flour a 13x9x2-inch baking dish; set aside. In a mixer bowl stir together the 2 cups flour, the 1½ cups sugar, baking soda, salt, cinnamon, nutmeg, and cloves. Add the reserved prune liquid and cooking oil. Beat on low speed of electric mixer till well combined. Add eggs, one at a time, beating on medium speed for 1 minute after each addition. Stir in chopped prunes. Turn batter into prepared baking dish.

For topping, in the *microwave oven* cook butter or margarine in a 1-cup glass measure, uncovered, on high power for 45 seconds or till melted. Add the ½ cup sugar and the 2 tablespoons all-purpose flour, stirring till the mixture resembles coarse crumbs.

Sprinkle the top of the cake batter with topping, then sprinkle with chopped walnuts. In the *conventional oven* bake at 350° about 40 minutes or till a wooden pick inserted near the center of cake comes out clean. Place cake on a wire rack, cool thoroughly. Makes 1 cake.

ORANGE-CHOCOLATE CAKE

4 squares (4 ounces) unsweetened chocolate
½ cup hot water
¼ cup sugar
2¼ cups sifted cake flour
1½ cups sugar
1 tablespoon baking powder
½ teaspoon salt
½ cup cooking oil
7 egg yolks
½ cup cold water
¼ cup orange liqueur
¾ cup flaked coconut
7 egg whites
½ teaspoon cream of tartar
Golden Butter Frosting

In the *microwave oven,* in a nonmetal bowl cook chocolate, uncovered, on high power for 2 to 3 minutes or till melted. Stir in the ½ cup hot water and the ¼ cup sugar; cool.

In a large mixing bowl stir together cake flour, the 1½ cups sugar, baking powder, and salt. Make a well in the center; add cooking oil, egg yolks, the ½ cup cold water, and orange liqueur. Beat on low speed of electric mixer till combined, beat on high speed about 5 minutes more or till satin smooth. Stir in chocolate mixture and coconut.

In a large mixing bowl, using clean beaters, beat egg whites and cream of tartar till stiff peaks form. Pour batter in a thin stream over entire surface of egg whites; fold in by hand. Turn into an ungreased 10-inch tube pan. In the *conventional oven* bake at 325° for 1 to 1¼ hours or till done. Invert to cool. Loosen cake; remove from pan. Frost with Golden Butter Frosting. Makes 1 cake.

Golden Butter Frosting: In the *microwave oven* cook ½ cup *butter or margarine*, uncovered, on high power about 3 minutes or till golden brown. Stir in 2 cups sifted *powdered sugar*. Blend in ¼ cup *light cream*. Stir in 2 cups more sifted *powdered sugar*. Stir 1 teaspoon *vanilla*. Blend in enough additional *light cream* (1 to 2 tablespoons) to make frosting of desired consistency.

CRANBERRY-NUT PUDDING

Freeze fresh cranberries when in season so you can make this dessert anytime of the year—

2½ cups fresh or frozen cranberries
⅔ cup packed brown sugar
⅓ cup water
½ cup all-purpose flour
½ teaspoon baking powder
¼ teaspoon ground allspice
⅓ cup sugar
⅓ cup butter or margarine, softened
1 egg
⅓ cup chopped walnuts
   Unsweetened whipped cream or pressurized dessert topping (optional)

In a 4-cup glass measure combine cranberries, brown sugar, and the water; cover with vented clear plastic wrap. In the *microwave oven* cook on high power for 4 to 5 minutes or till cranberries pop, stirring once during cooking. Divide the hot cranberry mixture evenly among eight 6-ounce custard cups.

In a mixing bowl stir together flour, baking powder, and ground allspice; set aside. In a small mixer bowl beat sugar and softened butter or margarine on medium speed of electric mixer till fluffy. Beat in egg. Add dry ingredients, beating on low speed till just combined. Fold in the chopped walnuts.

Spoon the batter over the cranberry mixture in each custard cup, dividing the batter evenly. Place the custard cups on a baking sheet or in a shallow baking pan. In the *conventional oven* bake at 350° for 18 to 20 minutes or till done. Top with whipped cream or pressurized dessert topping, if desired. Makes 8 servings.

GERMAN APPLE PANCAKE

1 tablespoon butter or margarine
2 eggs
¾ cup milk
2 tablespoons sugar
¾ cup all-purpose flour
⅛ teaspoon salt
1 tablespoon butter or margarine
2 large cooking apples, peeled, cored, and thinly sliced
⅓ cup raisins
1 tablespoon sugar
½ teaspoon ground cinnamon
½ cup apple cider or apple juice
1 teaspoon cornstarch
   Powdered sugar

For pancake, on the *range top,* melt 1 tablespoon butter or margarine in a 10-inch oven-going skillet, lifting and tilting to coat bottom and sides; set aside.

In a large mixer bowl beat eggs on high speed of electric mixer till foamy. Stir in milk and the 2 tablespoons sugar; add flour and salt, beating till smooth. Pour the mixture into the buttered skillet. In the *conventional oven* bake, uncovered, at 375° for 35 to 40 minutes or till puffed and golden brown.

Meanwhile, for sauce, place 1 table-spoon butter or margarine in a nonmetal mixing bowl. In the *microwave oven* cook, uncovered, on high power for 30 to 40 seconds or till melted. Stir in sliced apples, raisins, the 1 tablespoon sugar, and cinnamon. Combine apple cider or apple juice and cornstarch; stir into the apple mixture. Micro-cook, uncovered, on high about 3 minutes or just till apples are tender and the mixture is slightly thickened, stirring once during cooking.

Serve pancake from skillet or, using two spatulas, transfer pancake to a warm plate. Sprinkle powdered sugar over pancake. Cut into wedges; spoon warm apple sauce over each serving. Serve immediately. Makes 3 or 4 servings.

BAKED COFFEE-DATE PUDDING

This hearty date dessert resembles a steamed pudding. To enhance the mild coffee flavor of the pudding, top each serving with coffee ice cream—

2 cups water
8 ounces pitted whole dates, snipped (1½ cups)
1 cup sugar
½ cup cooking oil
1 tablespoon instant coffee crystals
½ teaspoon salt
½ teaspoon ground cinnamon
¼ teaspoon ground cloves
2 cups all-purpose flour
2 teaspoons baking soda
   Vanilla or coffee ice cream, slightly softened

In a 1½-quart nonmetal casserole combine the water, snipped pitted dates, sugar, cooking oil, instant coffee crystals, salt, cinnamon, and cloves. In the *microwave oven* cook date mixture, uncovered, on high power for 3 to 4 minutes or till the mixture is boiling and the sugar is dissolved, stirring once during cooking.

In a large mixing bowl stir together flour and baking soda; stir in the hot date mixture. Turn into an ungreased 8x1½-inch round baking dish. In the *conventional oven* bake at 325° for 30 to 40 minutes or till the pudding tests done.

Before serving, cut the dessert into wedges. Top each wedge with slightly softened vanilla or coffee ice cream. Serve warm. Makes 6 to 8 servings.

SWEET POTATO-APPLE PIE

2 medium sweet potatoes
   (about ¾ pound total)
2 medium apples, peeled, cored,
   and chopped (2 cups)
1 tablespoon water
1¼ cups all-purpose flour
½ teaspoon salt
⅓ cup shortening *or* lard
3 to 4 tablespoons cold water
2 slightly beaten eggs
1¼ cups milk
⅔ cup packed brown sugar
½ to 1 teaspoon ground cinnamon
¼ teaspoon salt
¼ teaspoon ground nutmeg
   Whipped cream (optional)

Wash and prick the sweet potatoes; place on paper toweling in the *microwave oven*. Cook sweet potatoes, uncovered, on high power for 7 to 9 minutes or till tender, rearranging once. Peel and mash the cooked sweet potatoes (you should have about 1 cup). Set aside.

Place apples and the 1 tablespoon water in a 1-quart nonmetal casserole. Micro-cook, covered, on high about 3 minutes or just till tender; drain well.

Meanwhile, for pastry, in bowl stir together flour and the ½ teaspoon salt. Cut in shortening or lard till pieces are the size of small peas. Sprinkle *1 tablespoon* of the cold water over part of the mixture; gently toss with a fork to moisten. Add remaining cold water, 1 tablespoon at a time, tossing till all is moistened. Form into a ball; flatten on a lightly floured surface. Roll out from center to edge, forming a circle 12 inches in diameter. Fit pastry into a 9-inch pie plate; trim. Flute edge high.

Place apples in pie plate. Combine eggs, milk, brown sugar, cinnamon, the ¼ teaspoon salt, nutmeg, and mashed sweet potato; beat with a rotary beater till smooth. Pour over apples. Cover edge of pastry with foil. In the *conventional oven* bake at 375° for 25 minutes. Remove foil; bake 20 to 25 minutes more or till a knife inserted just off-center comes out clean. Cool on a wire rack. Serve with whipped cream, if desired. Serves 8.

SPICY PEACH COBBLER

¾ cup all-purpose flour
¼ cup sugar
1 teaspoon baking powder
¼ teaspoon salt
1 beaten egg yolk
½ cup dairy sour cream
1 tablespoon butter *or* margarine,
   melted
¼ teaspoon finely shredded
   lemon peel
1 29-ounce can peach slices
2 tablespoons sugar
4 teaspoons cornstarch
1 teaspoon ground cinnamon *or*
   ½ teaspoon ground nutmeg
¼ cup butter *or* margarine
1 tablespoon lemon juice
½ teaspoon vanilla
   Chopped pecans (optional)
   Light cream (optional)

For batter, in a mixing bowl stir together flour, the ¼ cup sugar, baking powder, and salt. Combine egg yolk, sour cream, the 1 tablespoon melted butter or margarine, and shredded lemon peel; add to the flour mixture, stirring just till combined. Set batter aside.

Drain peach slices, reserving ¾ cup syrup. In a 1½-quart nonmetal casserole combine the 2 tablespoons sugar, cornstarch, and cinnamon or nutmeg; stir in the peach slices, the reserved syrup, and the ¼ cup butter or margarine.

In the *microwave oven* cook peach mixture, uncovered, on high power about 8 minutes or till thickened and bubbly, stirring three times during cooking. Stir in lemon juice and vanilla.

Immediately drop batter in 5 or 6 mounds atop the hot peach mixture. In the *conventional oven* bake at 350° for 35 to 40 minutes or till done. Sprinkle with chopped pecans, if desired. Serve warm. If desired, serve with light cream. Makes 5 or 6 servings.

MARLBOROUGH PIE

1¼ cups all-purpose flour
½ teaspoon salt
⅓ cup shortening *or* lard
3 to 4 tablespoons cold water
3 tart medium cooking apples,
   peeled, cored, and coarsely
   chopped (3 cups)
1 cup sugar
2 teaspoons finely shredded
   lemon peel
3 tablespoons lemon juice
4 beaten eggs
1 cup light cream
½ teaspoon ground cinnamon
1 medium apple, sliced and
   poached (optional)

For pastry, in a bowl stir together flour and salt. Cut in shortening or lard till pieces are the size of small peas. Sprinkle *1 tablespoon* of the water over part of the mixture; gently toss with a fork to moisten. Add the remaining water, 1 tablespoon at a time, tossing till all is moistened. Form into a ball; flatten on a lightly floured surface. Roll out from center to edge, forming a circle 12 inches in diameter. Fit pastry into a 9-inch nonmetal pie plate; trim. Flute edge high. Line pastry shell with waxed paper and fill with dry beans. In the *microwave oven* cook, uncovered, on high power for 3 minutes, giving the dish a half-turn once. Remove waxed paper and beans; micro-cook, uncovered, on high about 1 minute more or till pastry is dry. Set aside on a wire rack.

For filling, in a nonmetal 1½-quart casserole combine the chopped apples, sugar, lemon peel, and lemon juice. Micro-cook, covered, on high about 5 minutes or till sugar is dissolved and apples are very tender, stirring once. Puree the mixture in a blender or a food processor. Cool for 5 minutes. Combine eggs, light cream, cinnamon, and the pureed apple mixture; mix well. Pour into pastry shell.

In the *conventional oven* bake pie at 375° about 30 minutes or till set in center. Cool on wire rack. Just before serving, garnish with poached apple slices, if desired. Makes 8 servings.

ORANGE CUSTARDS WITH APRICOT SAUCE

- 4 slightly beaten eggs
- 2 cups milk
- ⅓ cup sugar
- 2 tablespoons orange liqueur (optional)
- 1 teaspoon finely shredded orange peel
  Dash salt
- 1 8¾-ounce can unpeeled apricot halves
- 2 tablespoons sugar
- 1½ teaspoons cornstarch

In a mixing bowl place eggs, milk, the ⅓ cup sugar, orange liqueur (if desired), finely shredded orange peel, and salt; beat with a rotary beater till combined. Divide mixture evenly among six 6-ounce custard cups or ½-cup individual molds. Place custard cups in a 13x9x2-inch baking dish. Pour boiling water into baking dish around custard cups to a depth of 1 inch. In the *conventional oven* bake at 325° for 25 to 30 minutes or till a knife inserted near the centers of the custards comes out clean. Cover and chill custards in the *refrigerator* up to 24 hours.

When ready to serve, prepare the sauce. Drain apricot halves, reserving the syrup. Slice the apricots; set aside. Add enough water to the reserved syrup to make ½ cup liquid. In a 2-cup glass measure combine the reserved apricot liquid, 2 tablespoons sugar, and cornstarch. Stir in sliced apricots. In the *microwave oven* cook, uncovered, on high power for 2 to 3 minutes or till thickened and bubbly; stirring twice during cooking. Cool slightly.

To unmold chilled custards, loosen edges with a spatula or knife; slip point of knife down sides to let in air. Invert the custards into individual dessert dishes. Spoon some of the apricot sauce over each custard. Makes 6 servings.

NUTTY CARAMEL APPLE COOKIES

- 2 cups all-purpose flour
- ½ teaspoon baking soda
- ½ teaspoon salt
- ½ teaspoon ground cinnamon
- 1 cup butter *or* margarine
- ½ cup sugar
- ½ cup packed brown sugar
- 1 egg
- 1 teaspoon vanilla
- 1½ cups peeled and shredded apple
- 10 vanilla caramels
- 2 tablespoons butter *or* margarine
- ½ cup sifted powdered sugar
  Milk
- ½ cup finely chopped walnuts

Lightly grease a cookie sheet; set aside. In a mixing bowl stir together flour, baking soda, salt, and ground cinnamon. In a large mixer bowl combine the 1 cup butter or margarine, sugar, and brown sugar; beat on medium speed of electric mixer till fluffy. Add egg and vanilla; beat well. Stir in the dry ingredients; fold in shredded apple.

Drop the cookie batter from a teaspoon onto the prepared cookie sheet. In the *conventional oven* bake at 375° for 10 to 12 minutes or till done. Remove from cookie sheet; cool the cookies on a wire rack before frosting.

For frosting, in a 2-cup glass measure combine unwrapped caramels and the 2 tablespoons butter or margarine. In the *microwave oven* cook the mixture, uncovered, on high power about 2 minutes or till melted, stirring once during cooking. Stir in powdered sugar. If mixture seems thick, stir in milk till of desired consistency (about 1 to 2 teaspoons). Stir in finely chopped walnuts.

Spread the caramel frosting over the cooled cookies. If frosting becomes too stiff, reheat, uncovered, in the *microwave oven* for ½ to 1 minute or till spreadable. Continue spreading frosting on the cookies. Makes about 48 cookies.

CHOCOLATE-NUT STRIPS

- ¾ cup all-purpose flour
- ½ cup whole wheat flour
- ½ teaspoon baking soda
  Dash salt
- 1 cup packed brown sugar
- ½ cup shortening
- ½ cup creamy *or* chunk-style peanut butter
- 1 egg
- 1½ cups milk chocolate pieces
- ½ cup finely chopped peanuts

In a mixing bowl stir together the all-purpose flour, whole wheat flour, baking soda, and salt. In a large mixer bowl combine the brown sugar, shortening, and creamy or chunk-style peanut butter; beat on medium speed of electric mixer till fluffy. Add egg; beat well. Add dry ingredients to the beaten mixture and beat till combined. Divide dough into four portions; wrap and chill in the *refrigerator* till firm enough to handle.

In a *microwave oven*, in a nonmetal mixing bowl cook milk chocolate pieces, uncovered, on high power about 1½ minutes or till melted, stirring after every 30 seconds.

On waxed paper roll out one portion of chilled dough into a 10x6-inch rectangle. Chill the dough rectangle in the *refrigerator*. Repeat rolling out a second portion of dough on waxed paper; spread with *half* of the melted milk chocolate. Sprinkle with *half* of the finely chopped peanuts. Invert the chilled dough rectangle onto the chocolate-nut layer; peel off the waxed paper; chill. Repeat with the remaining dough, chocolate and peanuts.

Cut each filled rectangle into thirty-two 3-inch-long strips. Place the strips on an ungreased cookie sheet. In a *conventional oven* bake at 350° for 8 to 10 minutes or till done. Remove cookies from cookie sheet; cool on a wire rack. Makes 64 cookies.

CHEESE-BACON APPETIZERS

You can make these appetizers ahead, then store them in the refrigerator till it's time to pop them in the oven—

- ¼ cup water
- 2 tablespoons dry sherry
- 2 tablespoons soy sauce
- ¼ teaspoon ground ginger
- 10 whole water chestnuts
- 10 slices bacon, halved
- 3 ounces Swiss cheese, cut into ½-inch cubes

For marinade, in a small mixing bowl combine the water, dry sherry, soy sauce, and ground ginger. Halve the water chestnuts crosswise. Add the water chestnut halves to the soy sauce marinade. Let stand in marinade at room temperature for at least 1 hour. Drain well, discarding the marinade.

Place the bacon slice halves between paper toweling on a paper plate. In the *microwave oven* cook the bacon slices on high power for 3½ to 4 minutes or till nearly done, rearranging pieces once during cooking.

To assemble, wrap one piece of bacon around a Swiss cheese cube and a water chestnut half; secure with a wooden pick. Repeat with the remaining bacon slice halves, cheese cubes, and water chestnut halves, making 20 appetizers. If desired, store in the *refrigerator* till serving time for up to 24 hours.

Place appetizers in a 12-inch pizza pan. In the *conventional oven* bake at 350° for 3 to 4 minutes or till the cheese cubes start to melt and the bacon is done. Makes 20 appetizers.

MEXICAN-STYLE STUFFED CHEESE

- 1 2-pound piece desired cheese (see options below)
- ½ of a 15-ounce can refried beans
- 1 small tomato, seeded and chopped
- 3 tablespoons canned green chili peppers, rinsed, seeded, and chopped
- 1 clove garlic, minced
- ¼ teaspoon dried oregano, crushed
- ¼ teaspoon ground coriander
- ¼ teaspoon bottled hot pepper sauce
  Cooking oil
  Tortilla chips

If cheese has a wax coating or rind, remove with a vegetable peeler. If cheese is rounded, cut a thin slice from the top of the cheese; invert cheese to stand on cut surface. Using a grapefruit knife and a spoon, hollow out the cheese, leaving a shell about ½ inch thick. Reserve the scooped-out cheese and the slice from the top.

For filling, in a nonmetal bowl combine the refried beans, chopped tomato, green chili peppers, garlic, oregano, coriander, and hot pepper sauce. In the *microwave oven* cook, uncovered, on high power for 3 to 4 minutes or till mixture is very hot, stirring once during cooking.

Brush the outside of the cheese lightly with some cooking oil. Place the cheese in a 1-quart casserole; spoon hot filling into cheese. Shred or crumble ¼ cup of the reserved scooped-out cheese; sprinkle over filling. (Cover and refrigerate any leftover cheese for another use.)

In the *conventional oven* bake at 350° for 10 to 15 minutes or till cheese starts to melt. Remove from oven. Serve immediately with tortilla chips. Makes 12 to 16 appetizer servings.

Cheese Options: Use a 2-pound round or rectangular block of cheddar, colby, Edam, fontina, Gouda, Monterey Jack, or provolone cheese cut about 3 inches thick.

FRESHENING SNACK CHIPS

The microwave oven can bring back crispness in tortilla and corn chips, potato chips, and pretzels.

Just spread 2 cups of chips in a shallow nonmetal baking dish. Micro-cook snack chips, uncovered, on high power about 1 minute. Let the hot chips stand for 1 to 2 minutes before serving.

SWISS CHEESE-DILL PUFFS

- ½ cup butter *or* margarine
- ¾ cup shredded process Swiss cheese (3 ounces)
- 1 tablespoon milk
- 1 teaspoon snipped chives
- ⅛ teaspoon dried dillweed
- 2 stiff-beaten egg whites
- 18 to 22 1-inch French bread cubes

In the *microwave oven*, in a 1-quart nonmetal casserole cook butter or margarine, uncovered, on high power for 1¼ to 2 minutes or till melted. Stir in shredded Swiss cheese, milk, snipped chives, and dillweed. Micro-cook, uncovered, for 1½ to 2 minutes or till cheese is melted, stirring mixture once during cooking. Gently fold in the stiff-beaten egg whites.

Dip bread cubes in the Swiss cheese mixture to coat. Place bread cubes on a greased baking sheet. In the *conventional oven* bake at 400° for 8 to 10 minutes or till golden brown. Serve hot. Makes 18 to 22 appetizers.

MICROWAVE
PLUS GRILL OR BROILER

Now you can speed up your cookout with a little help from your microwave oven. For Pear-Stuffed Pork Chops, the pear stuffing is micro-cooked. In Citrus-Yam Kabobs (see recipe, page 56), the vegetables and lemon glaze are precooked in the microwave oven before grilling.

If you savor the smoky aroma of a barbecue, you will be thrilled to see how your microwave oven fits into the picture. The microwave oven conveniently precooks many foods that normally require long grilling times. Thus, you save on coals and time, without sacrificing any flavor.

The microwave is handy for thickening glazes and sauces, as well as reheating them to serve along with your grilled pièce de résistance.

The barbecue grill and the broiler often are used interchangeably because both employ the same kind of heat. In several recipes in this chapter, you will see instructions given for both grilling and broiling.

In addition to cooking foods completely, the broiler will function as a browning unit to add a golden touch to microcooked dishes. You will also find it useful when you want to crisp a crumb topping or melt cheese atop a microcooked dish.

PEAR-STUFFED PORK CHOPS

 6 pork loin chops, cut 1½ inches thick
   Salt
   Pepper
 1 cup chopped, unpeeled pear *or* apple (1 medium)
 ½ cup chopped celery
 2 tablespoons sliced green onion
 2 tablespoons butter *or* margarine
 1 beaten egg
 1 cup toasted white *or* whole wheat bread cubes (1½ slices)
 ¼ teaspoon salt
 ⅛ teaspoon ground cloves
 ⅛ teaspoon pepper

Cut a pocket in each chop by cutting from fat side almost to bone edge. Season cavities with salt and pepper.

For stuffing, in a 1-quart nonmetal casserole combine the chopped pear or apple, celery, green onion, and butter or margarine. In the *microwave oven* cook, covered, on high power for 2 to 3 minutes or till tender.

In a medium mixing bowl combine the beaten egg, toasted white or whole wheat bread cubes, the ¼ teaspoon salt, ground cloves, and the ⅛ teaspoon pepper. Pour the cooked pear mixture over bread cube mixture; toss gently to mix.

Spoon about ⅓ *cup* of the stuffing into the pocket of *each* pork chop. Securely fasten the pocket openings with wooden picks.

On the *barbecue grill* grill the chops over *medium* coals for 20 minutes. Turn the meat and grill for 20 to 25 minutes more or till well-done. Before serving, remove wooden picks. Makes 6 servings.

SPICY BARBECUED SPARERIBS

Cut the time but not the flavor by precooking spareribs in the microwave oven—

 ¼ cup finely chopped onion
 2 tablespoons butter *or* margarine
 ½ cup chili sauce
 ¼ cup packed brown sugar
 ¼ cup lemon juice
 1 teaspoon salt
   Dash bottled hot pepper sauce
 3 pounds pork spareribs, cut into serving-size pieces

For sauce, in a small nonmetal mixing bowl combine the chopped onion and butter or margarine; cover tightly with vented clear plastic wrap. In the *microwave oven* cook on high power about 1½ minutes or till the onion is tender. Stir in the chili sauce, brown sugar, lemon juice, salt, and bottled hot pepper sauce; set the sauce aside.

Arrange the spareribs in a 12x7½x2-inch nonmetal baking dish, overlapping slightly as necessary; cover loosely with clear plastic wrap or waxed paper. Micro-cook on high for 10 minutes; drain off fat. Rearrange and turn ribs over, so the less-cooked pieces are exposed and the more-cooked portions of meat are overlapping. Micro-cook ribs, loosely covered, on high for 10 minutes more.

Transfer the partially cooked spareribs to the *barbecue grill.* Grill over *medium* coals about 15 minutes or till done, brushing often with sauce and turning the ribs occasionally during cooking. Makes 6 servings.

STEAK IN THYME SAUCE

4 **beef top loin steaks, cut 1 inch thick (about 2 pounds)**
Salt
Pepper
¼ **cup sliced green onion**
2 **tablespoons butter *or* margarine**
1 **clove garlic, minced**
½ **teaspoon dried thyme, crushed**
3 **tablespoons water**
1 **teaspoon instant beef bouillon granules**
1 **teaspoon Worcestershire sauce**
¼ **cup brandy**

Without cutting meat, slash the fat edges of steaks at 1-inch intervals. Place steaks on rack of unheated *broiler* pan. Broil steaks 3 inches from heat to desired doneness (allow 8 to 10 minutes total for rare, 12 to 14 minutes for medium, 18 to 20 minutes for well-done), turning after half the cooking time and sprinkling with salt and pepper. Transfer the steaks to a warm serving platter.

Meanwhile, for sauce, in a 1-cup glass measure combine green onion, butter or margarine, garlic, and thyme; cover tightly with vented clear plastic wrap. In the *microwave oven* cook on high power about 1½ minutes or till onion is tender. Stir in the water, beef bouillon granules, and Worcestershire sauce. Micro-cook, covered, on high about 1 minute more or till bouillon granules are dissolved, stirring once during cooking.

To serve, pour the sauce over the steaks. Micro-cook brandy, covered, on high about 1 minute or till hot. Carefully ignite the brandy. Pour the flaming brandy over steaks; allow the flame to subside. Makes 4 servings.

DUTCH-STYLE BRATWURST

4 **medium potatoes, peeled and quartered (about 1½ pounds)**
1 **medium onion, chopped**
½ **cup water**
1 **10-ounce package frozen chopped spinach**
2 **tablespoons water**
¼ **cup butter *or* margarine**
1 **teaspoon prepared horseradish**
½ **teaspoon salt**
⅛ **teaspoon pepper**
¼ **to ⅓ cup light cream *or* milk**
6 **fully cooked bratwurst, halved lengthwise**

Place potato pieces, onion, and the ½ cup water in a 10x6x2-inch nonmetal baking dish; cover tightly with vented clear plastic wrap. In the *microwave oven* cook on high power for 14 to 16 minutes or till tender, stirring once during cooking; remove and drain well.

Place frozen spinach and the 2 tablespoons water in the same baking dish; cover tightly with vented clear plastic wrap. Micro-cook on high for 5 to 7 minutes, stirring once during cooking. Let stand, covered, for 3 minutes. Drain well, squeezing out excess liquid.

In a mixing bowl combine the potato mixture and spinach. Beat on low speed of electric mixer till smooth. Add the butter or margarine, horseradish, salt, and pepper; beat till combined. Beat in enough light cream or milk to make fluffy.

On the *barbecue grill* grill bratwurst over *medium-hot* coals for 4 minutes. Turn and grill for 3 to 4 minutes more or till heated through. *(Or,* place bratwurst on rack of unheated *broiler* pan. Broil 3 to 5 inches from heat for 3 minutes. Turn and broil for 1 to 2 minutes more or till heated through.)

Meanwhile, spread the spinach mixture in the 10x6x2-inch nonmetal baking dish. In the *microwave oven* cook, loosely covered, on high power for 2 to 3 minutes or till heated through, giving the dish a half-turn once. Arrange bratwurst atop spinach mixture. Makes 6 servings.

GLAZED HAM WITH PEACH SAUCE

Leftover glaze serves as a base for the peach sauce—

1 **8¾-ounce can peach slices**
⅓ **cup bottled barbecue sauce**
¼ **cup sliced green onion**
¼ **cup apricot preserves**
1 **tablespoon cooking oil**
Several dashes bottled hot pepper sauce
1 **1½-pound fully cooked center-cut ham slice, cut 1 inch thick**

For glaze, drain the canned peach slices, reserving ⅓ cup of the syrup. Set peach slices aside.

In a 2-cup glass measure combine reserved peach syrup, barbecue sauce, sliced green onion, apricot preserves, cooking oil, and bottled hot pepper sauce. In the *microwave oven* cook, uncovered, on high power about 3 minutes or till boiling, stirring once or twice during cooking.

Trim the rind of ham slice, if present; slash the fat edge to prevent curling. On the *barbecue grill* grill the ham slice over *medium* coals for 10 to 15 minutes, brushing with the apricot glaze occasionally during cooking. Turn the ham and grill for 10 to 15 minutes more or till heated through, brushing occasionally with the glaze. *(Or,* place the ham on rack of unheated *broiler* pan. Broil the ham 3 inches from heat for 16 to 18 minutes or till heated through, turning once and brushing often with the glaze.)

For sauce, stir the peach slices into the remaining glaze. Return to the *microwave oven* and cook, uncovered, on high power about 3 minutes more or till heated through. To serve, spoon peach sauce over ham. Makes 6 servings.

Stuffing Burgers

Place eight of the meat patties on waxed paper. Spoon the potato stuffing in the center of one patty, as shown. Leave a margin of about ½ inch around the edge to help ensure that the stuffing stays inside the burger during cooking. Repeat with the remaining seven patties and stuffing.

Place one of the eight remaining plain patties atop each of the stuffing-topped patties, aligning the edges, as shown. With your fingers, press the edges of the patties together to seal. If necessary, gently reshape the stuffed burgers into circles with your hands.

POTATO-STUFFED BURGERS

1 cup shredded peeled potato (about 1 medium)
¼ cup chopped onion
¼ cup shredded carrot
2 tablespoons butter *or* margarine
1 beaten egg
⅓ cup fine dry bread crumbs
¼ teaspoon salt
¼ teaspoon dried marjoram, crushed
⅛ teaspoon pepper

2 beaten eggs
¼ cup fine dry bread crumbs
¼ cup milk
2 tablespoons snipped parsley
1 tablespoon Worcestershire sauce
1 teaspoon salt
Dash pepper
2 pounds ground beef
Catsup (optional)

For stuffing, in a 1-quart nonmetal casserole combine potato, onion, carrot, and butter or margarine. In the *microwave oven* cook, covered, on high power about 5 minutes or till tender, stirring once.

Combine the 1 beaten egg, the ⅓ cup dry bread crumbs, the ¼ teaspoon salt, marjoram, and the ⅛ teaspoon pepper; stir into the potato mixture.

For meat patties, in a mixing bowl combine the 2 beaten eggs, the ¼ cup fine dry bread crumbs, milk, parsley, Worcestershire sauce, the 1 teaspoon salt, and the dash pepper. Add the ground beef; mix well. Form the meat mixture into sixteen 4-inch patties.

To assemble, on waxed paper place about *2 tablespoons* stuffing atop *each* of 8 patties to within ½ inch of edges. Top with remaining patties; seal edges.

Place the stuffed burgers on the *barbecue grill*. Grill burgers over *medium* coals for 6 to 8 minutes. Turn and grill for 6 to 8 minutes more or to desired doneness. Serve with catsup, if desired. Makes 8 servings.

USING FOIL IN THE MICROWAVE OVEN

Check your manufacturer's instructions to see if you can use small amounts of foil in your microwave oven. Although large amounts of foil should not be used in any microwave oven, small pieces may be allowed in some for shielding. Used in this way foil protects portions of foods from overcooking, such as wing and drumstick tips on poultry.

If you are able to use small pieces of foil in your microwave oven, make sure that none of it touches the oven walls as this may cause arcing, or sparks.

TANGY BARBECUED CHICKEN

- 1 2½- to 3-pound broiler-fryer chicken, cut up
- ¼ cup apricot preserves
- ¼ cup Russian salad dressing
- 2 tablespoons regular onion soup mix

In a 10x6x2-inch nonmetal baking dish arrange chicken pieces, skin side up, with meatiest portions toward outside of dish. Cover loosely with waxed paper or clear plastic wrap. In the *microwave oven* cook on high power for 15 minutes or till partially cooked, giving the baking dish a quarter-turn after every 3 minutes.

Meanwhile, for glaze, in a small mixing bowl combine apricot preserves, Russian salad dressing, and soup mix.

Transfer the partially cooked chicken pieces to the *barbecue grill* and grill over *medium-hot* coals for 5 minutes. Brush glaze over chicken. Grill about 10 minutes more or till done, brushing occasionally with the glaze and turning pieces to brown evenly on all sides. Transfer to a serving platter. Makes 6 servings.

ORANGE CURRY CHICKEN

- 1 2½- to 3-pound broiler-fryer chicken, cut up
- 1 teaspoon finely shredded orange peel
- ¼ cup orange juice
- 2 tablespoons brown sugar
- 1 tablespoon snipped parsley
- 1 tablespoon curry powder
- 1 clove garlic, minced
- 1 teaspoon minced dried onion
- ½ teaspoon salt
- ⅛ teaspoon pepper
  Plain yogurt (optional)

Rinse chicken pieces; pat dry with paper toweling. For marinade, combine orange peel, orange juice, brown sugar, parsley, curry powder, garlic, dried onion, salt, and pepper.

Place the chicken pieces in a large plastic bag set in a deep bowl. Pour the marinade over chicken. Close bag; marinate in the *refrigerator* for 6 hours or overnight, turning the bag occasionally to coat chicken evenly.

Remove chicken pieces, reserving the marinade. Place the chicken pieces in a 12x7½x2-inch nonmetal baking dish, skin side down, with the meatiest portions toward outside of dish. Cover loosely with clear plastic wrap or waxed paper. In the *microwave oven* cook the chicken on high power for 10 minutes, giving the dish a half-turn once during cooking.

Transfer chicken to rack of unheated *broiler* pan; brush with reserved marinade. Broil 4 to 5 inches from heat for 5 to 7 minutes or till tender. Serve with yogurt, if desired. Makes 6 servings.

LEMON-GINGER TURKEY

- 1 9- to 11-pound fresh *or* frozen turkey
- ¼ cup butter *or* margarine
- ¼ cup teriyaki sauce
- 2 tablespoons lemon juice
- 2 tablespoons bottled barbecue sauce
- 2 teaspoons grated gingerroot
- ¼ teaspoon pepper

Thaw turkey, if frozen. In the *microwave oven*, in a 2-cup glass measure cook butter or margarine, uncovered, on high power about 1 minute or till melted. Stir in teriyaki sauce, lemon juice, barbecue sauce, gingerroot, and pepper.

Rinse turkey; pat dry. Rub cavity with butter mixture. Skewer neck skin to back. Tie legs together and wings close to body. Cover tips of wings and legs with small pieces of foil (see tip, upper left). Place, breast side down, on inverted saucers in a 12x7½x2-inch nonmetal baking dish. Brush with butter mixture. Cover loosely with waxed paper.

Micro-cook turkey on high for 24 minutes for a 9-pound bird; 30 minutes for an 11-pound bird. Give dish a half-turn after half the cooking time. Turn, breast side up; brush with butter mixture. Micro-cook, covered, on high for 12 minutes more for a 9-pound bird; 15 minutes more for an 11-pound bird. Give dish a half-turn during cooking. Insert a microwave meat thermometer in center of inside thigh muscle. Micro-cook, covered, on high till thermometer registers 140° (allow about 12 minutes for a 9-pound bird; about 15 minutes for an 11-pound bird). Remove thermometer; brush bird with butter mixture.

Meanwhile, in the covered *barbecue grill* arrange *medium-slow* coals around a heavy foil drip pan. Place turkey on grill over drip pan. Insert a conventional meat thermometer. Lower grill hood. Grill over *medium-slow* coals for 1½ to 2 hours or till thermometer registers 180° to 185°. Brush often with butter mixture; add more coals, if necessary. Cover bird with foil. Let stand 15 minutes before carving. Makes 10 to 12 servings.

CORNISH HENS WITH PEPPERONI STUFFING

Pictured on pages 4 and 5—

4 cups hickory chips
4 ounces pepperoni, finely chopped
¼ cup water
4 slices raisin bread, toasted and cubed (2½ cups)
¼ teaspoon ground nutmeg
1 medium apple, chopped (1 cup)
2 tablespoons apple juice
2 tablespoons butter or margarine, melted
4 1- to 1½-pound Cornish game hens
Cooking oil
Seedless green grapes (optional)
Apricots, halved (optional)
Chive flowers (optional)

About 1 hour before grilling, soak hickory chips in enough water to cover.

For stuffing, in a 2-cup glass measure combine pepperoni and the ¼ cup water. In the *microwave oven* cook, covered, on high power for 2 minutes. Drain. In a mixing bowl combine bread cubes and nutmeg. Stir in the pepperoni and apple. Sprinkle with apple juice and melted butter or margarine. Toss gently to mix.

Rinse hens; pat dry. Skewer neck skin to back. Fill each body cavity with about ¾ cup stuffing. Tie legs securely to tail; twist wing tips under back.

Arrange hens, breast side down, on a large nonmetal platter. Brush with cooking oil. Cover loosely with waxed paper. Micro-cook on high for 15 minutes, giving the dish a quarter-turn every 3 minutes.

In the covered *barbecue grill* arrange *medium-hot* coals around a heavy foil drip pan. Sprinkle coals with dampened chips.

Place birds, breast side up, on grill over drip pan, allowing space between each bird. Lower grill hood; grill over *medium-hot* coals about 30 minutes or till tender, brushing birds often with cooking oil. Transfer birds to platter; if desired, garnish with green grapes, apricot halves, and chive flowers. Serves 8.

SCALLOPS ON A SKEWER

8 ounces fresh or frozen scallops
3 tablespoons butter or margarine
1 tablespoon orange marmalade
1 tablespoon lemon juice
1 tablespoon soy sauce
¼ teaspoon ground ginger
1 medium green pepper, cut into 1-inch squares
12 slices bacon, halved crosswise

Thaw scallops, if frozen. For marinade, in a 2-cup glass measure combine butter or margarine, orange marmalade, lemon juice, soy sauce, and ginger. In the *microwave oven* cook, uncovered, on high power for 1 to 2 minutes or till butter or margarine is melted, stirring once during cooking.

Place scallops in a mixing bowl; pour marinade atop. Cover and let stand at room temperature for 30 minutes. Drain scallops, reserving marinade.

Meanwhile, in a small nonmetal mixing bowl micro-cook the green pepper squares, covered, on high for 2 minutes; set aside.

Place *half* of the bacon on a paper plate between 2 layers of paper toweling. Micro-cook on high about 2½ minutes or till bacon is partially cooked. Repeat with remaining bacon.

Wrap each scallop with a partially cooked bacon piece. On six skewers thread the bacon-wrapped scallops alternately with green pepper squares, securing bacon with skewer and allowing some space between each scallop and green pepper square.

On the *barbecue grill* grill over *hot* coals for 4 minutes. Turn, using spatula; brush with the reserved marinade. Grill for 4 to 6 minutes more or till bacon is crisp and brown, and scallops are done. Makes 6 servings.

SEAFOOD THERMIDOR

8 ounces fresh or frozen fish fillets
2 6-ounce frozen lobster tails
¾ cup dry white wine
¼ cup chopped onion
¼ cup chopped celery
1 bay leaf
1 teaspoon dry mustard
1 teaspoon paprika
1 cup sliced fresh mushrooms
½ cup milk
3 tablespoons all-purpose flour
2 tablespoons snipped parsley
1 teaspoon instant chicken bouillon granules
¾ cup soft bread crumbs
2 tablespoons grated Parmesan cheese
2 tablespoons butter or margarine, melted

Thaw fish, if frozen. On the *range top* cook lobster tails for 8 minutes in enough boiling salted water to cover. Drain and cool. Place, shell side down, on cutting board. Cut in half lengthwise. Remove lobster meat; cut into chunks. Clean and reserve shell halves.

In a 12x7½x2-inch nonmetal baking dish combine wine, onion, celery, bay leaf, mustard, paprika, and ¾ cup *water*. Arrange fish in dish, thicker parts toward outside. In the *microwave oven* cook, covered, on high power for 4 to 5 minutes or till fish flakes easily, giving dish a half-turn after 3 minutes. Remove fish, reserving liquid; cut fish into cubes. Strain the liquid.

Return ¾ cup reserved liquid to dish. Add mushrooms; micro-cook, covered, on high for 1 minute. Combine milk and flour; add to mushrooms. Stir in parsley and bouillon granules. Micro-cook, uncovered, on high about 5 minutes or till bubbly, stirring after every minute. Stir in lobster and fish; spoon into shell halves. Arrange in a broiler-proof 13x9x2-inch baking pan. Add extra mixture to pan.

Combine bread crumbs, Parmesan cheese, and butter or margarine; sprinkle atop. Under *broiler* broil 5 inches from heat about 2 minutes or till brown. Serve immediately. Makes 4 servings.

ORIENTAL-STYLE STUFFED FISH

- 2 1½-pound fresh *or* frozen dressed whitefish, perch, trout, catfish, *or* Spanish mackerel (with head removed)
  Hickory chips
- 1⅔ cups water
- ⅔ cup brown rice
- ¼ teaspoon salt
- ½ cup sliced carrot
- ¼ cup snipped chives
- 2 tablespoons butter *or* margarine
- 1 tablespoon lime juice
- 1 tablespoon soy sauce
- 1 clove garlic, minced
- 1 teaspoon grated gingerroot
- 1 tablespoon sesame seed, toasted

Thaw fish, if frozen. One hour before cooking, soak the hickory chips in enough water to cover.

For stuffing, on the *range top* combine the 1⅔ cups water, brown rice, and salt in a medium saucepan; bring to boiling. Reduce heat; cover and simmer for 40 to 45 minutes or till water is absorbed. (Rice will be chewy.)

Meanwhile, in a 4-cup glass measure combine the carrot, chives, butter or margarine, lime juice, soy sauce, garlic, and gingerroot; cover tightly with vented clear plastic wrap. In the *microwave oven* cook on high power for 5 to 6 minutes or till carrot is tender, stirring twice during cooking. Stir in the sesame seed and cooked rice. Sprinkle fish cavity with salt, if desired. Spoon stuffing into fish cavity.

Drain hickory chips. In the covered *barbecue grill* arrange *slow* coals around edge of grill. Sprinkle some dampened hickory chips generously over coals. Center a greased heavy-duty foil pan on grill, not directly over the coals. Place fish in the foil pan. Close grill hood. Grill over *slow* coals for 50 to 60 minutes or till fish flakes easily when tested with a fork. Sprinkle additional hickory chips over the coals after every 20 minutes. Transfer the fish to a serving platter. Garnish with parsley and carrot curls, if desired. Makes 6 servings.

SOUFFLÉ-TOPPED SALMON

- 1 10-ounce package frozen asparagus *or* broccoli spears
- 1 tablespoon water
- 1 15½-ounce can salmon, drained, broken into chunks, and skin and bones removed
- ⅔ cup mayonnaise *or* salad dressing
- ⅔ cup desired shredded *or* grated cheese* (about 3 ounces)
- ½ teaspoon finely shredded lemon peel
- 4 egg whites
- ¼ teaspoon cream of tartar
- ¼ teaspoon salt
  Desired shredded *or* grated cheese* (optional)
- 2 tablespoons sliced almonds

In a broiler-proof 12x7½x2-inch non-metal baking dish place asparagus or broccoli spears and water. Cover tightly with vented clear plastic wrap. In the *microwave oven* cook on high power for 4 to 6 minutes or till vegetables are crisp-tender, separating and rearranging the spears once during cooking. Drain.

Sprinkle salmon atop vegetables in baking dish. Micro-cook, covered, on high for 1 to 2 minutes or till salmon is heated through.

For topping, in a mixing bowl combine the mayonnaise or salad dressing, the ⅔ cup desired shredded or grated cheese, and lemon peel. In a large mixing bowl combine egg whites, cream of tartar, and salt; beat on high speed of electric mixer till stiff peaks form (the tips stand straight). Fold in mayonnaise mixture.

Spread the topping over the salmon and vegetables; sprinkle with the additional cheese, if desired. Under the *broiler* broil 3 to 5 inches from heat for 3 to 5 minutes or till golden brown. Sprinkle sliced almonds atop. Serve immediately. Makes 4 servings.

*Cheese options: Select shredded cheddar, American, Gruyère, provolone, Havarti, Edam, fontina, or grated Parmesan or Romano cheese.

PEPPER-STUFFED ARTICHOKES

Grill these flavorful artichokes along with your choice of meat—

- 2 medium artichokes
  Lemon juice
- ¼ cup water
- 1 cup chopped fresh mushrooms
- ¼ cup chopped green pepper
- 2 tablespoons butter *or* margarine
- 1½ cups soft bread crumbs (2 slices)
- ¼ cup grated Parmesan cheese
- 2 tablespoons snipped parsley
- ¼ teaspoon dried oregano, crushed
  Few drops bottled hot pepper sauce

Remove the stems and loose outer leaves from artichokes. Cut 1 inch from tops of artichokes; using scissors, snip off sharp leaf tips. Brush cut edges with lemon juice. Place artichokes and water in a 2-quart nonmetal casserole. In the *microwave oven* cook, covered, on high power for 9 to 13 minutes or till a leaf pulls out easily, giving dish a half-turn once during cooking. Drain the artichokes and set aside till cool enough to handle.

For stuffing, in the casserole combine the mushrooms, green pepper, and butter or margarine. Micro-cook, covered, on high for 2 to 3 minutes or till tender. Add bread crumbs, Parmesan cheese, parsley, oregano, and hot pepper sauce; toss gently to mix.

Spread the artichoke leaves slightly. Spoon stuffing into center of each artichoke and behind each leaf.

Wrap the stuffed artichokes tightly in two 10-inch squares of foil. On the *barbecue grill* grill over *medium* coals about 20 minutes or till heated through. Makes 2 side-dish servings.

Soufflé-Topped Salmon

CITRUS-YAM KABOBS

Pictured on page 48—

- 2 medium yams *or* sweet potatoes
- 1 10-ounce package frozen brussels sprouts
- 8 small onions
- 2 tablespoons water
- ½ of a 6-ounce can frozen lemonade concentrate, thawed (⅓ cup)
- ¼ cup chili sauce
- 1 teaspoon prepared mustard

Wash, prick, and place the yams or sweet potatoes on paper toweling in the *microwave oven.* Micro-cook, uncovered, on high power for 5 to 9 minutes, rearranging once. Let stand for 3 minutes. Peel; cut into bite-size chunks. Set aside.

In a 1-quart nonmetal casserole combine frozen brussels sprouts, onions, and water. Micro-cook, covered, on high for 5 to 6 minutes, stirring once during cooking. Let stand, covered, for 3 minutes. Cut any large brussels sprouts in half. Set aside.

For glaze, in a 2-cup glass measure combine the lemonade concentrate, chili sauce, and mustard. Micro-cook, uncovered, on high about 1 minute or till the mixture is heated through.

On 4 skewers alternately thread the sweet potato or yam chunks, brussels sprouts, and onions; brush with glaze. On the *barbecue grill* grill over *medium* coals for 20 to 25 minutes or till done, turning and brushing often with glaze. Serves 4.

CARAWAY GRILLED POTATOES

- 2 large baking potatoes
  Salt
- ¼ cup butter *or* margarine
- ¼ cup finely chopped green onion
- 1 teaspoon caraway seed
- ¼ teaspoon dry mustard

Wash, prick, and place potatoes on paper toweling in the *microwave oven.* Micro-cook, uncovered, on high power for 4 minutes or till partially cooked, rearranging once during cooking. Cut each potato crosswise into ¼-inch-thick slices. Sprinkle with salt.

In a nonmetal bowl micro-cook butter or margarine, uncovered, on high about 40 seconds or till melted. Stir in green onion, caraway seed, and dry mustard.

Brush the cut surfaces of the potatoes with the butter mixture; reassemble potatoes and wrap tightly in foil.

On the *barbecue grill* grill over *medium* coals about 20 minutes or till done. Makes 2 to 3 servings.

PARMESAN-GARLIC BREAD

- ¼ cup butter *or* margarine
- 1 clove garlic, minced
- ¼ cup grated Parmesan cheese
- 2 tablespoons snipped parsley
- 8 hard rolls

In a 2-cup glass measure combine butter or margarine and garlic. In the *microwave oven* cook, uncovered, on high power for ½ to 1 minute or till butter is melted. Stir in Parmesan cheese and parsley.

Split each roll lengthwise, cutting to, but not through, opposite side of roll. Spread with Parmesan mixture; close rolls. Wrap rolls loosely in heavy foil.

On the *barbecue grill* grill wrapped rolls over *medium* coals for 8 to 10 minutes or till heated through, turning once. Makes 8 servings.

RHUBARB AND APPLE CRISP

The topping for this taste-tempting dessert turns crisp and golden under the broiler—

- ½ cup packed brown sugar
- 1 teaspoon ground cinnamon
- ¼ teaspoon salt
- 1 20-ounce can sliced apples, drained
- 2 cups sliced rhubarb
- ½ cup all-purpose flour
- ½ cup quick-cooking rolled oats
- ¼ cup packed brown sugar
- ⅓ cup butter *or* margarine
  Whipped cream *or* vanilla ice cream (optional)

In a mixing bowl combine the ½ cup brown sugar, cinnamon, and salt. Add the drained apple slices and sliced rhubarb; toss gently to coat. Let the mixture stand for 5 minutes.

Turn the apple-rhubarb mixture into a broiler-proof 10x6x2-inch nonmetal baking dish; cover loosely with waxed paper or clear plastic wrap. Cook in the *microwave oven* on high power about 8 minutes or till rhubarb is tender, stirring gently after half the cooking time.

For topping, in a medium mixing bowl combine flour, rolled oats, and the ¼ cup brown sugar. Cut in the butter or margarine till mixture resembles coarse crumbs. Sprinkle the topping over the apple-rhubarb mixture in baking dish.

Under the *broiler* broil the dessert 4 to 5 inches from heat about 2 minutes or till the topping is golden. Serve warm. If desired, top each serving with a dollop of whipped cream or a scoop of vanilla ice cream. Makes 6 servings.

RASPBERRY MERINGUE PIE

1 9-inch frozen unbaked pastry shell
2 cups fresh *or* frozen red raspberries
¾ cup sugar
1 tablespoon quick-cooking tapioca
1 pint vanilla ice cream
3 egg whites
⅓ cup sugar

Bake the pastry shell in the *conventional oven* according to package directions. Cool to room temperature.

Thaw raspberries, if frozen. In a 2-quart nonmetal casserole crush the berries with a potato masher; stir in the ¾ cup sugar and tapioca. Let stand for 15 minutes.

In the *microwave oven* cook the raspberry mixture, uncovered, on high power about 5 minutes or till bubbly, stirring after every minute. Cool slightly, then chill in the *refrigerator* till cold.

To soften the vanilla ice cream, in a mixing bowl stir ice cream with wooden spoon and press against the side of bowl. Soften till just pliable. Using a metal spatula, spread the ice cream in the cooled, baked pastry shell. Spread the chilled raspberry mixture atop. Cover and place in the *freezer* for several hours or till the mixture is firm.

For meringue, in a medium mixing bowl beat egg whites on high speed of electric mixer till soft peaks form (tips curl over). Gradually add the ⅓ cup sugar, about 1 tablespoon at a time, beating about 4 minutes more or till stiff peaks form (tips stand straight).

Immediately spread meringue atop frozen raspberry mixture, sealing to edge of pastry crust. Under the *broiler* broil 4 to 5 inches from heat for 1 to 2 minutes or till meringue is golden. Serve immediately. Makes 8 servings.

APPLE-STRAWBERRY BRÛLÉ

A brûlé is a dish with a caramelized sugar topping—

4 medium apples, cored and sliced
2 tablespoons water
2 cups sliced fresh strawberries
1 4-ounce container whipped cream cheese
¾ cup dairy sour cream
1 tablespoon brown sugar
2 tablespoons brown sugar

In a 9-inch nonmetal pie plate combine the apple slices and water; cover tightly with vented clear plastic wrap. In the *microwave oven* cook the apple slices on high power about 5 minutes or till tender, stirring gently once during cooking. Drain the apple slices and cool to room temperature.

If desired, reserve *3* of the strawberry slices for a garnish. Spread the remaining strawberry slices atop the cooled apple slices in the pie plate.

For topping, in a mixing bowl beat the cream cheese on high speed of electric mixer till fluffy. Add the sour cream and the 1 tablespoon brown sugar; beat till smooth. Spoon the cream cheese topping over the strawberry slices.

Sprinkle the 2 tablespoons brown sugar evenly over the cream cheese topping. Under the *broiler* broil 4 to 5 inches from heat for 1 to 2 minutes or till the brown sugar is bubbly. Arrange the reserved strawberry slices atop the dessert, if desired. Serve immediately. Makes 8 servings.

TESTING THE COALS

To determine if your coals are the right temperature, hold your hand palm-side down above the coals at the height the food will be cooking. Begin counting "one thousand one, one thousand two"; if you need to withdraw your hand after two seconds the coals are hot, three seconds for medium-hot, four seconds for medium, and five or six seconds for slow.

GRILLED SHERRY BANANA SPLITS

1 square (1 ounce) unsweetened chocolate
2 tablespoons sugar
2 tablespoons orange juice
1 tablespoon cream sherry
4 medium bananas, peeled
1 cup sliced fresh strawberries *or* pineapple chunks
  Frozen whipped dessert topping, thawed
¼ cup chopped walnuts
4 maraschino cherries

For sauce, in a 1-cup glass measure cook chocolate in the *microwave oven*, uncovered, on high power for 2 to 2½ minutes or till melted, stirring once.

Stir sugar, juice, and sherry into chocolate. Micro-cook, uncovered, on high for 30 to 45 seconds or till dissolved. Stir till combined.

Slice bananas lengthwise. Place *two* halves, side by side, atop *each* of four 12x8-inch pieces of foil. Place *¼ cup* strawberries or pineapple atop *each* pair. Pour chocolate sauce atop fruit. Wrap in foil pieces. Place on the *barbecue grill.* Grill over *medium* coals for 20 to 25 minutes or till heated through.

Open wrapping and garnish with topping, walnuts, and cherries. Serves 4.

MICROWAVE
PLUS REFRIGERATOR

The refrigerator performs a necessary function in Garden Salad Pie (see recipe, page 60). After dissolving the lime-flavored gelatin in the microwave oven, you need to chill the gelatin mixture in the refrigerator before adding the shredded carrot and zucchini and the cottage cheese layer.

Although you may not think of your refrigerator as a cooking appliance, it is often involved in the cooking process. Prime examples include setting up a gelatin mixture, marinating meat and vegetables, or chilling a food that needs to be served cold.

Sometimes you will want to partially prepare a dish the day before you serve it, leaving only some last-minute steps and the final cooking for the next day. The refrigerator provides an excellent place to store most of these dishes. You'll find several recipes throughout this chapter that may be held in the refrigerator for up to 24 hours. These make-ahead recipes will come in handy if you anticipate a relatively busy day ahead.

CORNED BEEF AND CABBAGE MOLDS

Pictured on pages 4 and 5—

- 1 medium potato
- 2 envelopes unflavored gelatin
- 2 tablespoons sugar
- 2 teaspoons instant beef bouillon granules
- ⅓ cup vinegar
- ⅓ cup mayonnaise *or* salad dressing
- ⅓ cup dairy sour cream
- ½ teaspoon salt
- 1 cup finely chopped cabbage
- ¼ cup finely chopped onion
- 1 teaspoon prepared horseradish
- 1 12-ounce can corned beef, flaked
- ¼ cup finely chopped green pepper

Wash, prick, and place the potato on paper toweling in the *microwave oven.* Cook, uncovered, on high power for 3 to 4 minutes; let stand 5 minutes. Peel and finely chop.

In a 4-cup glass measure soften gelatin in 1 cup warm *water.* Stir in the sugar and bouillon granules. Micro-cook, uncovered, on high for 2 to 2½ minutes or till dissolved, stirring once. Stir in 2 cups *water* and the vinegar. Reserve *2 cups* of the gelatin mixture; do not chill.

In a mixing bowl combine the mayonnaise or salad dressing, sour cream, and salt; gradually stir in the remaining gelatin mixture. In the *refrigerator* chill mayonnaise mixture till it is the consistency of unbeaten egg whites (partially set).

Fold cabbage, onion, and potato into mayonnaise mixture; spoon into seven 1-cup molds or one 7-cup mold. In the *refrigerator* chill the mixture till *almost* firm.

For second layer, stir horseradish into the reserved 2 cups gelatin mixture; chill till partially set. Fold in corned beef and green pepper; carefully spoon atop the mayonnaise mixture. In the *refrigerator* chill for several hours or overnight till firm. Unmold; garnish with shredded cabbage, if desired. Makes 6 or 7 servings.

GAZPACHO CHICKEN

- 1 cup water
- 1 large tomato
- ½ cup chopped cucumber
- ¼ cup chopped green pepper
- 2 tablespoons chopped onion
- 1 clove garlic, minced
- 1 tablespoon lemon juice
- ½ teaspoon sugar
- ¼ teaspoon salt
- ¼ teaspoon pepper
- 2 whole medium chicken breasts, skinned, halved lengthwise, and boned
  Salt
- 2 tablespoons tomato paste

In a 2-cup glass measure place the water. In the *microwave oven* cook, covered, on high power for 1 to 2 minutes or till boiling. Spear tomato with a fork; dip into hot water for 12 seconds. Hold the tomato under cold running water till cool enough to handle; remove and discard the peel and seeds. Coarsely chop the tomato (you should have 1 cup).

In a medium mixing bowl combine the chopped tomato, cucumber, green pepper, onion, garlic, lemon juice, sugar, the ¼ teaspoon salt, and the pepper.

Arrange the chicken pieces in a 1½-quart nonmetal casserole, placing the meatiest portions toward the outside of casserole. Sprinkle with the additional salt. Pour tomato mixture atop chicken. Cover and chill in the *refrigerator* for 3 hours or overnight.

Before serving, in the *microwave oven* cook the casserole, covered, on high power for 16 to 20 minutes or till the chicken is tender, rearranging chicken pieces once during cooking.

For sauce, remove chicken pieces; stir the tomato paste into tomato mixture in the casserole. Micro-cook, uncovered, on high about 1 minute more or till heated through and blended. Serve the sauce over chicken. Makes 4 servings.

COOLING FOODS BEFORE CHILLING

Hot foods that need to be chilled should not be left at room temperature to cool first. And since large volumes of hot food can raise the temperature inside the refrigerator, cool hot food quickly by placing it in a shallow container and setting the container in a pan of ice water.

VEAL MARSALA

1 pound veal leg round steak, cut ¼ inch thick
Salt
Pepper
¼ cup dry marsala *or* sherry
2 tablespoons water
2 tablespoons sliced green onion
¼ teaspoon dried basil, crushed

Cut veal into 4 pieces. Place 1 piece of veal between 2 pieces of clear plastic wrap. Pound with a meat mallet to about ⅛-inch thickness, working from center to edges. Remove plastic wrap; sprinkle meat with salt and pepper. Repeat with the remaining veal. Place the veal in an 8x8x2-inch nonmetal baking dish.

In a small mixing bowl combine the dry marsala or sherry, water, green onion, and basil. Pour over veal. Cover tightly with clear plastic wrap and chill in the *refrigerator* for 3 hours or overnight.

Fold plastic wrap back slightly at edge of dish to vent. In the *microwave oven* cook, covered, on high power for 1 minute. Turn the veal and micro-cook, covered, on high about 3 minutes more or till the veal is done. Transfer to a warm serving platter. Makes 4 servings.

SOLE WITH WALNUTS

1 16-ounce package frozen sole *or* other fish fillets
¼ cup water
¼ cup dry white wine
2 lemon slices, halved
½ teaspoon salt
¼ teaspoon dried tarragon, crushed
⅛ teaspoon pepper
3 medium carrots, thinly sliced
2 tablespoons water
1 medium zucchini, thinly sliced
1 tablespoon water
2 tablespoons butter *or* margarine,
⅓ cup chopped walnuts

Let frozen fish stand at room temperature for 20 minutes. Cut the fish fillets crosswise into 4 serving-size portions. Arrange the fish portions in a 12x7½x2-inch nonmetal baking dish.

For marinade, combine the ¼ cup water, the wine, halved lemon slices, salt, tarragon, and pepper. Pour over fish. Cover and marinate in the *refrigerator* for 3 hours or overnight, spooning the marinade over the fish occasionally.

Meanwhile, in a 1½-quart nonmetal casserole combine the carrot slices and the 2 tablespoons water. In the *microwave oven* cook, covered, on high power for 2 minutes. Add zucchini slices and the 1 tablespoon water. Micro-cook, covered, on high about 1 minute more or till vegetables are crisp-tender. Drain well; cover and chill in the *refrigerator* for 3 hours or overnight.

Before serving, remove the lemon slices from the fish; drain off marinade. In the *microwave oven* cook butter or margarine, uncovered, on high power for 30 to 40 seconds or till melted. Drizzle the butter or margarine over fish. Add the carrot-zucchini mixture. Sprinkle with walnuts. Cover with vented clear plastic wrap and micro-cook on high for 6 to 9 minutes or till fish flakes easily when tested with a fork, giving the dish a half-turn once during cooking. Makes 4 servings.

GARDEN SALAD PIE

Pictured on page 58—

1 3-ounce package lime-flavored gelatin
1 cup water
1 8½-ounce can (½ cup) applesauce
1 teaspoon finely shredded lemon peel, set aside
2 tablespoons lemon juice
½ cup shredded zucchini
½ cup shredded carrot
2 tablespoons finely chopped green pepper
2 tablespoons thinly sliced green onion
1 cup dry cottage cheese
½ cup dairy sour cream
¼ teaspoon salt
Dash white pepper
Shredded zucchini (optional)
Shredded carrot (optional)

In a 4-cup glass measure combine the lime-flavored gelatin and water. In the *microwave oven* cook, uncovered, on high power about 1½ minutes or till gelatin is dissolved, stirring once during cooking. Stir in the applesauce and lemon juice. Chill the mixture in the *refrigerator* till it is the consistency of unbeaten egg whites (partially set).

Fold in the ½ cup shredded zucchini, the ½ cup shredded carrot, chopped green pepper, and sliced green onion. Turn the mixture into a lightly oiled 9-inch pie plate. Chill in the *refrigerator* till firm.

In a mixing bowl combine the lemon peel, cottage cheese, sour cream, salt, and white pepper. Spread the cottage cheese mixture atop the firm gelatin layer in the pie plate. Chill in the *refrigerator* till serving time. Garnish with the additional shredded zucchini and carrot, if desired. Makes 6 side-dish servings.

ORANGE-CIDER SALAD MOLD

1¾ cups apple cider *or* apple juice
2 whole cloves
2 inches stick cinnamon, broken
1 3-ounce package orange-
    flavored gelatin
1 11-ounce can mandarin orange
    sections, drained
1 medium apple, cored and
    chopped
    Shredded lettuce (optional)
    Seeded, halved grapes (optional)

In a 4-cup glass measure combine the apple cider or juice, cloves, and cinnamon; cover with vented clear plastic wrap. In the *microwave oven* cook on high power for 6 minutes. Strain mixture, discarding cloves and cinnamon.

Stir the orange-flavored gelatin into the hot cider. Micro-cook, covered, on high about 1 minute or till gelatin is dissolved, stirring once during cooking.

Pour ½ *cup* of the gelatin mixture into a 3-cup ring mold. Chill in the *refrigerator* till the mixture is the consistency of unbeaten egg whites (partially set). Do not chill the remaining gelatin mixture.

Arrange the mandarin orange sections in the partially set layer in the mold; chill in the *refrigerator* till *almost* firm.

Meanwhile, chill the remaining gelatin mixture till it is the consistency of unbeaten egg whites (partially set). Fold in the chopped apple. Carefully pour the apple-gelatin mixture over the almost-firm layer in the mold. Chill in the *refrigerator* for several hours or overnight till firm.

Unmold the salad onto a serving plate. Fill the center of molded salad with shredded lettuce and halved grapes, if desired. Makes 6 servings.

BRUSSELS SPROUTS IN WINE MARINADE

The brussels sprouts soak up the wine and herb flavor while marinating in the refrigerator—

1 10-ounce package frozen
    brussels sprouts
2 medium carrots, thinly sliced
2 tablespoons water
⅓ cup salad oil
¼ cup dry white wine
¼ cup vinegar
2 tablespoons sliced green onion
1 tablespoon Italian seasoning
1 tablespoon snipped parsley
2 teaspoons sugar
⅛ teaspoon pepper
    Lettuce leaves (optional)

Place frozen brussels sprouts, carrot slices, and water in a 1-quart nonmetal casserole. Cover and cook in the *microwave oven* on high power for 5 to 7 minutes or till the vegetables are crisp-tender, stirring once during cooking. Let stand, covered, for 3 minutes; drain. Halve any large brussels sprouts.

Meanwhile, for marinade, in a screw-top jar combine the salad oil, dry white wine, vinegar, sliced green onion, Italian seasoning, snipped parsley, sugar, and pepper. Cover the jar tightly and shake well to mix.

Pour the white wine marinade over the cooked brussels sprouts and carrots. Cover and chill in the *refrigerator* for at least 3 hours or overnight. Drain the vegetable mixture or serve with a slotted spoon. Serve on lettuce leaves, if desired. Makes 4 servings.

CUTTING VEGETABLES INTO EQUALLY SIZED PIECES

Fresh vegetables such as brussels sprouts will cook more evenly in the microwave if they are uniformly sized and shaped. Irregularly sized vegetable pieces have a tendency to overcook and become mushy in spots before some other areas are fully cooked.

QUICK 'N' EASY CORN RELISH

Serve this refreshing relish as an accompaniment to cold meats—

2 12-ounce cans whole kernel corn
    with sweet peppers, drained
3 tablespoons cooking oil
½ cup sugar
½ cup vinegar
2 teaspoons minced dried onion
½ teaspoon salt
¼ teaspoon celery seed

In a mixing bowl combine the drained corn and cooking oil; set aside.

In a 2-cup glass measure combine the sugar, vinegar, minced dried onion, salt, and celery seed; cover with vented clear plastic wrap. Cook in the *microwave oven* on high power for 1½ to 2 minutes or till boiling.

Stir the hot mixture into the corn mixture; cover and cool quickly in a pan of ice water. Chill the cooled mixture in the *refrigerator* for several hours or overnight. To serve, drain or serve with a slotted spoon. Makes about 3 cups.

ORANGE SHERBET SALAD

1 6-ounce package *or* two 3-ounce packages orange-flavored gelatin
2 cups water
2 tablespoons lemon juice
1 pint orange sherbet
1 15½-ounce can crushed pineapple
1 11-ounce can mandarin orange sections
½ cup sugar
1 envelope unflavored gelatin
1 beaten egg
1 cup whipping cream

In a 4-cup glass measure combine the orange-flavored gelatin and the water. In the *microwave oven* cook, uncovered, on high power about 2 minutes or till gelatin is dissolved, stirring once during cooking. Stir in the lemon juice. Add the orange sherbet by spoonfuls, stirring till melted. Chill in the *refrigerator* till mixture is the consistency of unbeaten egg whites (partially set).

Drain pineapple and mandarin orange sections, reserving 1 cup syrup. Fold the drained pineapple and orange sections into partially set sherbet mixture. Turn into a 12x7½x2-inch dish. Chill in the *refrigerator* till *almost* firm.

Meanwhile, prepare next layer. In a 2-cup glass measure combine sugar and unflavored gelatin. Stir in reserved syrup. In the *microwave oven* cook, uncovered, on high power for 2 to 2½ minutes or till gelatin is dissolved, stirring once during cooking. Add *some* of the hot mixture to beaten egg; return all to glass measure. Micro-cook, uncovered, on high for 30 seconds more. Cool thoroughly but do not allow mixture to set.

In a mixing bowl beat the whipping cream on high speed of an electric mixer till soft peaks form. Fold the cooled egg mixture into the whipped cream.

Spread the whipped cream mixture over the chilled sherbet mixture. Chill in the *refrigerator* till firm. Garnish with additional mandarin orange sections, if desired. Makes 12 servings.

TOMATO-POTATO SALAD

3 medium potatoes (1 pound)
½ cup mayonnaise *or* salad dressing
1 tablespoon red wine vinegar
½ teaspoon salt
¼ teaspoon dried basil, crushed
⅛ teaspoon pepper
1 7½-ounce can tomatoes, drained and cut up
2 hard-cooked eggs, chopped
½ cup sliced celery
¼ cup chopped onion
¼ cup chopped green pepper
¼ cup sweet pickle relish
  Lettuce leaves (optional)
  Hard-cooked egg wedges (optional)

Wash, prick, and place potatoes on paper toweling in the *microwave oven*. Cook, uncovered, on high power for 8 to 10 minutes or till almost done, rearranging potatoes once during cooking. Let stand for 5 minutes.

Meanwhile, for dressing, in a small mixing bowl stir together the mayonnaise or salad dressing, red wine vinegar, salt, basil, and pepper.

Peel and cube the cooked potatoes. In a large mixing bowl combine the potato pieces, tomatoes, the 2 chopped hard-cooked eggs, celery, onion, green pepper, and sweet pickle relish.

Pour the dressing over potato mixture; toss gently to coat. Cover and chill in the *refrigerator* for several hours or overnight. If desired, serve in lettuce-lined bowls and top each serving with additional hard-cooked egg wedges. Makes 5 or 6 servings.

POPPY SEED DESSERT

½ cup butter *or* margarine
½ cup all-purpose flour
½ cup finely crushed saltine crackers (14 crackers)
½ cup finely crushed graham crackers (7 crackers)
½ cup finely chopped black walnuts
1 cup sugar
¼ cup poppy seed
3 tablespoons cornstarch
1 envelope unflavored gelatin
2 cups milk
4 beaten egg yolks
1 teaspoon vanilla
4 egg whites
½ teaspoon cream of tartar
½ cup sugar

For crust, in the *microwave oven* cook butter or margarine in a 12x7½x2-inch nonmetal baking dish, uncovered, on high power for 1¼ to 2 minutes or till melted. Stir in flour, crushed crackers, and walnuts. Press firmly against bottom and sides of dish. Micro-cook, uncovered, on high for 1 to 3 minutes or till set, giving dish a half-turn twice; cool slightly.

In a 4-cup glass measure combine the 1 cup sugar, poppy seed, cornstarch, and gelatin. Stir in milk. Micro-cook, uncovered, on high about 7 minutes or till bubbly, stirring several times. Gradually stir *some* of the hot mixture into egg yolks. Return all to glass measure. Micro-cook, uncovered, on high for 1 minute more, stirring after every 20 seconds. Stir in vanilla. Cover and chill in the *refrigerator* till mixture is the consistency of unbeaten egg whites (partially set).

Beat egg whites and cream of tartar till soft peaks form (tips curl over). Gradually add the ½ cup sugar, beating till stiff peaks form (tips stand straight).

Fold the beaten egg whites into the gelatin mixture. Turn into the crust. Cover and chill in the *refrigerator* for several hours or overnight. Makes 12 servings.

Tomato-Potato Salad

Assembling Layered Fruit Dessert

To make a scalloped edge, fold a 9-inch circle of paper in half. Fold into quarters, then into eighths. Cut a rounded point at wide end. Unfold.
Place the paper pattern atop one pastry circle. Using a sharp paring knife, trace around the scalloped edge of paper pattern, as shown. (Or, trim pastry circles with a pastry wheel.)

Reserve ⅓ cup cherry filling for garnish. Spoon half of the remaining cherry filling atop one pastry circle to within 1 inch of edge, as shown. Use the remaining cherry filling and another pastry circle to form the bottom layer of a second stack. Work with one pastry circle while the next pastry circle is cooking in the microwave oven.

For each stack, place one cooked pastry circle atop the cherry mixture. Then spread half of the pineapple topping atop each pastry circle. Cover each stack with a large bowl to chill. Before serving, garnish each stack with drained peach slices and reserved cherry mixture, as shown. To serve, cut the layered fruit desserts with a serrated knife.

LAYERED FRUIT DESSERT

**Pastry for Double-Crust Pie
(see recipe, page 33)**
1 **21-ounce can cherry pie filling**
¼ **teaspoon ground cinnamon**
1 **package 4-serving-size instant
vanilla pudding mix**
1 **cup milk**
1 **tablespoon lemon juice**
1 **8¼-ounce can crushed
pineapple, drained**
½ **of a 4½-ounce container frozen
whipped dessert topping,
thawed**
1 **8¾-ounce can peach slices,
drained**

Prepare Pastry for Double-Crust Pie; divide into four portions. On a lightly floured surface roll each portion into a circle about 9 inches in diameter. Make scalloped edge using a paper pattern, if desired. Prick with fork.

Place the pastry circles on pieces of waxed paper. In the *microwave oven*, cook circles, one at a time, uncovered, on high power for 2½ to 3 minutes or till dry, giving the pastry a half-turn after half of the cooking time.

For cherry filling, combine cherry pie filling and cinnamon; set aside.

For pineapple topping, prepare vanilla pudding according to package directions, *except* use only 1 cup milk; add lemon juice. Fold in pineapple and dessert topping; set aside.

To make one stack, place one pastry circle on a serving plate. Reserve ⅓ cup of the cherry filling; spoon *half* of the remaining cherry filling to within 1 inch of pastry edge. Cover with a second pastry circle. Spread *half* of the pineapple topping atop. Make another stack by layering the remaining pastry circles, cherry filling, and pineapple topping. Cover and chill in the *refrigerator* for several hours.

Before serving, garnish each stack with peach slices and the reserved cherry filling. Makes 12 servings.

RASPBERRY CHARLOTTE

1 10-ounce package frozen red
   raspberries, thawed
1 cup water
1 3-ounce package raspberry-
   flavored gelatin
1 pint vanilla ice cream
1 3-ounce package (12) ladyfingers
   Whipped cream (optional)
   Toasted coconut (optional)

Drain the thawed raspberries, reserving syrup; set berries aside. In a
large nonmetal mixing bowl combine the
reserved syrup, water, and raspberry-fla-
vored gelatin. In the *microwave oven*
cook, uncovered, on high power for 2 to
3 minutes or till gelatin is dissolved, stirring once during cooking. Add the vanilla
ice cream by spoonfuls, stirring to melt.
Stir in the drained raspberries. Chill in the
refrigerator till the mixture is the consistency of unbeaten egg whites (partially
set).

Line the bottom of an 8x4x2-inch
loaf pan with waxed paper. Split lady fingers. Reserve three of the split ladyfingers; line the bottom and sides of loaf
pan with remaining split ladyfingers.

Spoon *half* of the partially set gelatin
mixture into the loaf pan. Arrange the
reserved ladyfingers atop. Spoon remaining gelatin mixture over all. If necessary, trim ends of the ladyfingers
arranged on the sides so they are level
with the filling. Cover and chill in the *refrigerator* overnight or till firm.

To serve, loosen sides with a spatula. Invert the dessert onto a serving
platter. Remove waxed paper. Slice the
loaf crosswise. If desired, top each serving with whipped cream and toasted coconut. Makes 6 servings.

FLUFFY APRICOT-PRUNE PIE

   Vanilla Wafer Crust
⅓ cup finely snipped dried apricots
⅓ cup finely snipped pitted, dried
   prunes
⅓ cup sugar
1½ teaspoons unflavored gelatin
1 teaspoon finely shredded orange
   peel
⅔ cup orange juice
2 eggs, separated
⅓ cup whipping cream

Prepare Vanilla Wafer Crust. In a 4-
cup glass measure combine apricots
and prunes. Pour in water to 1 inch
above fruit. In the *microwave oven* cook,
covered, on high power for 3 minutes.
Drain; cool.

In a 1½-quart nonmetal casserole
combine *half* of the sugar, the gelatin,
and ¼ teaspoon *salt*. Stir in the orange
peel and orange juice; micro-cook, uncovered, on high about 2 minutes or till
gelatin is dissolved, stirring once. Add
some of the gelatin mixture to slightly
beaten egg yolks; return all to the casserole. Micro-cook, uncovered, on high for
2 minutes more or till mixture thickens
slightly, stirring after every 30 seconds.
Chill gelatin mixture in the *refrigerator* till
it is the consistency of unbeaten egg
whites (partially set), stirring occasionally. Fold fruit into gelatin mixture.

Beat egg whites till soft peaks form.
Gradually add the remaining sugar, beating till stiff peaks form. Fold egg whites
into the gelatin mixture. Whip cream till
soft peaks form; fold into gelatin mixture.
Turn the mixture into cooled wafer crust.
Chill in the *refrigerator* for at least 6 hours
or overnight till firm. Makes 8 servings.

Vanilla Wafer Crust: In the *microwave oven* cook ⅓ cup *butter or margarine* in an uncovered 9-inch nonmetal pie
plate on high power about 1 minute or till
melted. Add 1¼ cups finely crushed *vanilla wafers* and 3 tablespoons *sugar;* stir
till all is moistened. Press firmly against
bottom and sides of pie plate. Micro-
cook, uncovered, on high for 1 to 3 minutes or till set, giving dish a half-turn once
or twice during cooking. Cool.

CHOCOLATE FLOATING ISLANDS

2 egg whites
¼ teaspoon cream of tartar
¼ cup sugar
3 cups milk
¾ cup semisweet chocolate pieces
½ cup sugar
2 egg yolks
2 eggs
1 teaspoon vanilla
2 teaspoons shortening

For meringue, in a mixing bowl beat
egg whites and cream of tartar till soft
peaks form (tips curl over). Gradually
add the ¼ cup sugar, beating till stiff
peaks form (tips stand straight).

Meanwhile, in the *microwave oven*
cook milk in a 12x7½x2-inch nonmetal
baking dish, covered, on high power for 6
to 8 minutes or till heated through.

Divide the meringue into 6 portions;
drop each portion onto the hot milk. Micro-cook, uncovered, on high for 1½ to 2
minutes or till meringues are firm, giving
dish a half-turn once during cooking. Lift
meringues from milk with a slotted spoon
and drain on paper toweling; chill in the
refrigerator.

In a 2-quart saucepan combine the
hot milk and ½ *cup* of the semisweet
chocolate pieces. On the *range top* cook
and stir over low heat till chocolate is
melted. Stir in the ½ cup sugar.

Beat together egg yolks and whole
eggs; gradually stir about *half* of the
chocolate mixture into eggs. Return all to
pan. Cook and stir over medium heat till
mixture coats a metal spoon. Remove
from heat; cool at once by placing saucepan in a bowl of ice water; stir for 1 to 2
minutes. Stir in vanilla. Turn into a serving bowl. Cover; chill in *refrigerator.*

For topping, in a 2-cup glass measure combine remaining chocolate
pieces and shortening. In the *microwave
oven* cook, uncovered, on high power
about 2 minutes or till melted, stirring
once.

To serve, arrange meringues atop
chilled egg mixture. Drizzle topping over
meringues. Makes 6 servings.

MICROWAVE
PLUS FREEZER

The microwave oven contributes the pecan crust and the tangy cranberry topping for this irresistible Frozen Cranberry Torte (see recipe, page 73). Your freezer steps in to take it from there.

One candidate for preparing food in conjunction with your microwave oven is the freezer. In this chapter, we've introduced several surprising uses for your freezer.

Make-ahead recipes appear as they did in the refrigerator chapter except, with the help of the freezer, you may prepare the food several weeks in advance of serving. You'll discover a frozen meat base from which you make three different main dishes using the microwave oven. You'll even find a frozen drink mix that just requires the additions of water and rum before heating in the microwave.

Some recipes, such as Orange-Rhubarb Freeze on page 72, utilize freezing as a key part of the preparation process. In this recipe, the rhubarb mixture is partially frozen, then beaten to incorporate air, thus improving the overall texture of the finished dessert.

BASIC FROZEN MEAT BASE

Simmer this savory meat base on the range top, then freeze it. You can use this frozen base to make Beef Paprikash, Applesauce-Beef Pie, and Tortilla-Beef Casserole. You'll find Basic Frozen Meat Base pictured on page 69—

- 4 pounds beef round steak, cut into ¾-inch pieces
- 2 tablespoons cooking oil
- 1 cup chopped onion
- 1 cup water
- ½ cup chopped green pepper
- 2 tablespoons instant beef bouillon granules
- 1 20-ounce package frozen crinkle-cut carrots
- 1 16-ounce package frozen cut green beans

On the *range top*, in a 12-inch skillet cook the meat, *one-third* at a time, in hot cooking oil till brown on all sides. Return all of the meat to the skillet.

Stir chopped onion, water, green pepper, and beef bouillon granules into the meat in the skillet. Bring the mixture to boiling; reduce heat. Cover and simmer over low heat about 1 hour or till the meat is tender, stirring the mixture occasionally during cooking.

Cool the meat mixture quickly by setting the skillet in a large shallow pan of ice water. Stir in the frozen crinkle-cut carrots and green beans.

Spoon *one-fourth* of the cooled meat mixture (about 3½ cups) into each of four 2-pint freezer containers. Seal the containers tightly and label. Store in the *freezer* till ready to use (up to 6 months). Makes 4 (3½-cup) portions.

BEEF PAPRIKASH

- 1 3½-cup portion Basic Frozen Meat Base
- ¼ cup water
- ¾ cup dry red *or* white wine
- 1 tablespoon paprika
- 1 bay leaf
- ½ teaspoon dried savory, crushed
- ¼ teaspoon salt
- ½ cup dairy sour cream
- 2 tablespoons all-purpose flour
  Spaetzle *or* noodles

To thaw Basic Frozen Meat Base, place the frozen mixture and the water in a 1½-quart nonmetal casserole. In the *microwave oven* cook, covered, on high power for 7 minutes. Break up the mixture with a fork. Micro-cook, covered, on high about 2 minutes more or till the mixture is completely thawed.

Stir in the red or white wine, paprika, bay leaf, savory, and salt. Micro-cook, covered, on high about 5 minutes more or till the vegetables in the frozen mixture are tender, stirring once during cooking.

In a small mixing bowl combine the sour cream and flour. Stir *some* of the hot liquid from the meat mixture into the sour cream mixture. Return all to casserole. Micro-cook, uncovered, on high about 4 minutes more or till thickened and bubbly, stirring after every minute. Remove and discard the bay leaf.

Meanwhile, on the *range top* cook spaetzle or noodles according to package directions; drain.

Serve the thickened meat mixture over the hot cooked spaetzle or noodles. Makes 6 servings.

APPLESAUCE-BEEF PIE

Pastry for Double-Crust Pie (see recipe, page 33)
1 **3½-cup portion Basic Frozen Meat Base (see recipe, page 67)**
¼ **cup water**
1 **8-ounce can unsweetened applesauce**
¼ **cup hot-style catsup**
3 **tablespoons all-purpose flour**
1½ **teaspoons poultry seasoning**
¼ **teaspoon salt**
1 **slightly beaten egg**

Prepare Pastry for Double-Crust Pie; form dough into 2 balls. To thaw the Basic Frozen Meat Base, place the mixture and the water in a 1½-quart nonmetal casserole. In the *microwave oven* cook, covered, on high power for 7 minutes. Break up the mixture with a fork; micro-cook, covered, on high about 2 minutes more.

In a mixing bowl stir together the applesauce, catsup, flour, poultry seasoning, and salt; stir into casserole. Micro-cook, uncovered, on high about 8 minutes or till thickened and bubbly, stirring after every 2 minutes. Micro-cook, uncovered, on high for 1 minute more, stirring once.

On a lightly floured surface roll one ball of pastry dough from center to edge, forming a circle about 12 inches in diameter; place in a 9-inch pie plate. Spoon meat mixture into crust. For top crust, roll remaining pastry dough into a circle 10 inches in diameter. Cut into 6 triangles. Arrange atop the meat mixture with points toward center; fold outside edges under bottom crust. Flute edge; brush pastry with beaten egg.

Bake in the *conventional oven* at 375° for 30 to 35 minutes or till done. Let stand 10 minutes before serving. Makes 6 servings.

TORTILLA-BEEF CASSEROLE

1 **3½-cup portion Basic Frozen Meat Base (see recipe, page 67)**
¼ **cup water**
1 **8¾-ounce can whole kernel corn, drained**
1 **8-ounce can tomato sauce**
1 **cup shredded sharp cheddar cheese (4 ounces)**
1 **cup broken tortilla chips**
½ **cup sliced pitted ripe olives**
¼ **cup taco sauce**
2 **teaspoons snipped fresh coriander *or* ½ teaspoon ground coriander (optional)**
1 **teaspoon sugar**
1 **teaspoon chili powder**
½ **teaspoon ground cumin**
½ **cup shredded sharp cheddar cheese (2 ounces)**
½ **cup broken tortilla chips**

To thaw the Basic Frozen Meat Base, place mixture and the water in a 2-quart nonmetal casserole. In the *microwave oven* cook, covered, on high power for 7 minutes. Break up the mixture with a fork; micro-cook, covered, on high about 2 minutes more.

Stir in the corn, tomato sauce, the 1 cup shredded cheddar cheese, the 1 cup tortilla chips, ripe olives, taco sauce, coriander, sugar, chili powder, and cumin. Micro-cook, uncovered, on high about 10 minutes or till vegetables in meat base are tender and mixture is heated through, stirring once during cooking.

Sprinkle the casserole with the ½ cup shredded cheddar cheese and the ½ cup tortilla chips. Micro-cook, uncovered, on high about 1 minute more or till cheese is melted. Makes 6 servings.

STUFFED SQUASH

1 **medium acorn squash, halved and seeded**
½ **pound ground beef**
2 **tablespoons chopped onion**
2 **tablespoons chopped green pepper**
1 **small tomato, peeled and chopped**
2 **tablespoons sliced pitted ripe olives**
1 **tablespoon butter *or* margarine**
½ **teaspoon Italian seasoning**
2 **to 4 tablespoons milk**
¼ **cup shredded mozzarella cheese**

Place squash halves, cut side down, in a 10x6x2-inch nonmetal baking dish; cover. In the *microwave oven* cook on high power for 5½ to 8 minutes, giving the dish a half-turn once during cooking. Let stand for 3 to 5 minutes or till tender.

In a 1-quart nonmetal casserole combine ground beef, onion, and green pepper. Micro-cook, covered, on high about 4 minutes or till meat is brown. Drain off fat.

Reserving squash shells, scoop out the insides; mash. Stir in tomato, olives, butter, Italian seasoning, ½ teaspoon *salt,* and dash *pepper.* Beat in enough milk to make fluffy. Stir meat mixture into squash mixture; spoon into shells. Cool.

Wrap each in moisture-vaporproof wrap; seal and label. Store in the *freezer* till ready to use (up to 3 months).

Before serving, unwrap and place stuffed squash in a 10x6x2-inch nonmetal baking dish. In the *microwave oven* cook, covered, on high power for 12 to 15 minutes or till heated through, giving dish a half-turn once during cooking. Sprinkle *each* half with *2 tablespoons* of the shredded cheese. Micro-cook, uncovered, on high about 30 seconds more or till cheese is melted. Makes 2 servings.

Applesauce-Beef Pie, Basic Frozen Meat Base (see recipe, page 67), and Tortilla-Beef Casserole

Pounding and Stuffing Chicken Breasts

Place each chicken breast half, boned side up, between two pieces of clear plastic wrap to prevent perforating the chicken. Using the fine-toothed side of a meat mallet, pound each piece of chicken to ⅛-inch thickness, working from center to edges, as shown. If a meat mallet is not available, pound the chicken with the broad side of a chef's knife or cleaver.

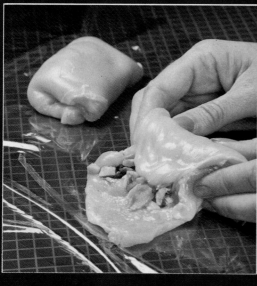

Remove the top piece of plastic wrap. Sprinkle the boned side of each chicken breast half with salt and pepper. Place 2 tablespoons filling on the seasoned side of each chicken breast half. Fold the long sides over part of the filling and roll up the chicken jelly-roll style, starting from a narrow end, as shown. Make sure the two folded sides are included in the roll to prevent the filling from falling out. Press all edges together gently with your fingers to seal.

CHICKEN ROLLS AMANDINE

  4 **slices bacon**
 ⅓ **cup chopped fresh mushrooms**
  1 **tablespoon snipped chives**
 ¼ **cup chopped almonds, toasted**
 ¼ **teaspoon dried thyme, crushed**
  1 **whole large chicken breast, skinned, halved lengthwise, and boned**
    Plain yogurt *or* **dairy sour cream**
    Sliced almonds, toasted
    Snipped chives
    Paprika

For filling, place the bacon slices in a 10x6x2-inch nonmetal baking dish; cover loosely with waxed paper. Cook in the *microwave oven* on high power about 4 minutes or till crisp. Drain off fat, reserving 2 tablespoons drippings in the baking dish. Drain the bacon on paper toweling; crumble and set aside.

Add the chopped mushrooms and the 1 tablespoon snipped chives to reserved drippings in dish. Micro-cook, covered, on high for 45 to 60 seconds or till tender. Stir in bacon pieces, the ¼ cup chopped almonds, and thyme.

Place each chicken breast half between two pieces of clear plastic wrap. Pound with a meat mallet to ⅛-inch thickness, working out from center to edges. Sprinkle one side of each chicken breast half with salt and pepper.

Place about *2 tablespoons* of the filling on the seasoned side of *each* chicken piece. Fold in sides; roll up jelly-roll style. Wrap chicken rolls in moisture-vaporproof wrap. Seal, label, and store in the *freezer* till ready to use (up to 3 months).

Before serving, thaw the chicken rolls. In the *microwave oven* cook chicken rolls in a 9-inch nonmetal pie plate, uncovered, on high power for 3 to 5 minutes or till chicken is done, giving the dish a half-turn once during cooking. Spoon yogurt or sour cream over each roll. Sprinkle with the sliced almonds, the additional chives, and paprika. Makes 2 servings.

FROZEN CURRY SAUCE

1 **large onion, chopped (1 cup)**
1 **cup chopped celery**
2 **cloves garlic, minced**
3 **tablespoons curry powder**
½ **cup butter** *or* **margarine**
⅓ **cup cornstarch**
2 **tablespoons instant chicken bouillon granules**
1 **6-ounce can tomato paste**
3½ **cups water**
1 **8½-ounce can applesauce**

On the *range top*, in a large saucepan cook the chopped onion, celery, garlic, and curry powder in hot butter or margarine about 10 minutes or till vegetables are tender.

Stir the cornstarch and chicken bouillon granules into vegetable mixture. Add the tomato paste; stir till combined. Stir in the water and applesauce. Cook and stir till the mixture is thickened and bubbly; cook and stir for 2 minutes more. Remove from heat; cool curry mixture quickly by setting saucepan in large pan of ice water, stirring occasionally.

Pour *one-fourth* of the cooled mixture (about 1½ cups) into each of four 2-cup freezer containers. Seal tightly and label the containers. Store in the *freezer* till ready to use (up to 6 months). Makes 4 (1½-cup) portions.

To serve, place one (1½-cup) portion *Frozen Curry Sauce* into a 1½-quart nonmetal casserole. In the *microwave oven* cook, covered, on high power for 5 to 7 minutes or till thawed, breaking up with fork once or twice to hasten thawing. Stir in 2½ cups diced cooked *meat, poultry, or fish* and ⅓ cup *plain yogurt*. Micro-cook, uncovered, on high for 1 to 2 minutes or till the mixture is heated through. Serve over hot cooked *rice or noodles*. Makes 6 servings.

CREOLE-STYLE CRAB

For entertaining, you can make these individual seafood casseroles ahead, then pop them into the microwave oven when your guests arrive—

1 **cup chopped onion**
1 **cup chopped celery**
½ **cup chopped green pepper**
¼ **cup butter** *or* **margarine**
2 **6- *or* 7-ounce cans crab meat, drained, flaked, and cartilage removed**
¾ **cup soft bread crumbs (1 slice)**
¼ **cup water**
2 **tablespoons snipped parsley**
1 **tablespoon lemon juice**
½ **teaspoon Creole Seasoning Mix (see recipe, page 33)**
¼ **cup crushed rich round crackers**

In a 2-quart nonmetal casserole combine onion, celery, green pepper, and butter or margarine. In the *microwave oven* cook, covered, on high power about 6 minutes or till the vegetables are tender, stirring once during cooking.

Stir in the crab meat, soft bread crumbs, water, parsley, lemon juice, and Creole Seasoning Mix.

Spoon the mixture into 4 coquille shells or four 10-ounce nonmetal au gratin dishes. Cover each tightly with moisture-vaporproof wrap. Seal and label. Store in the *freezer* till ready to use (up to 3 months).

Before serving, in the *microwave oven* cook the frozen casseroles, covered, on high power for 10 minutes. Sprinkle each casserole with crushed crackers and rearrange the shells or dishes. Micro-cook, uncovered, on high for 6 to 8 minutes more or till the casseroles are heated through. Makes 4 servings.

VEGETABLES WITH BASIL-CHEESE SAUCE

1½ **cups halved brussels sprouts**
2 **tablespoons water**
1½ **cups cauliflower flowerets**
1 **tablespoon butter** *or* **margarine**
1 **tablespoon all-purpose flour**
¼ **teaspoon dried basil, crushed**
⅛ **teaspoon pepper**
¾ **cup milk**
⅓ **cup shredded American cheese (about 1½ ounces)**

In a 1-quart nonmetal casserole combine the halved brussels sprouts and the water. In the *microwave oven* cook, covered, on high power for 2 minutes. Add the cauliflower flowerets and micro-cook, covered, on high for 3 to 4 minutes more or till the vegetables are crisp-tender. Drain well and set aside.

In the same casserole micro-cook the butter or margarine, uncovered, on high for 35 to 45 seconds or till melted. Stir in the flour, basil, and pepper. Stir in the milk; micro-cook, uncovered, on high for 2 to 3 minutes or till thickened and bubbly, stirring twice during cooking. Micro-cook, uncovered, on high for 1 minute more, stirring after 30 seconds.

Add the shredded cheese, stirring till melted. Add the cooked vegetables; stir gently to coat the vegetables with the cheese mixture.

Turn the mixture into a freezer container or a nonmetal freezer-to-microwave oven casserole. Cover and seal tightly; label. Store in the *freezer* till ready to use (up to 6 months).

Before serving, place the frozen mixture in a 1-quart nonmetal casserole or use freezer-to-microwave oven casserole. In the *microwave oven* cook the frozen mixture, covered, on high power for 6 to 8 minutes or till heated through, stirring once or twice during cooking. Makes 4 side-dish servings.

Making Orange-Rhubarb Freeze

Pour the cooked rhubarb mixture into a blender container or food processor bowl. Cover and blend or process till smooth. Add the orange liqueur or crème de cassis and the red food coloring, if desired. Cover and blend or process till combined. The mixture will be slightly thick with a few visible flecks of rhubarb, as shown.

Break the frozen rhubarb mixture into chunks with a wooden spoon, as shown. Transfer the broken-up mixture to a chilled large mixing bowl. The chunks should be small enough for easy mixing with an electric mixer. Keep the container chilled while beating the frozen rhubarb mixture.

Beat the frozen mixture on medium speed of electric mixer till smooth and fluffy; do not let the mixture melt. While beating, scrape mixing bowl with a rubber spatula. Beating the mixture before it is completely frozen incorporates air, which improves the consistency. Return the mixture to the chilled container, as shown. Cover and freeze till firm.

ORANGE-RHUBARB FREEZE

With a little help from the microwave oven, the blender and freezer turn rhubarb into an icy summer refresher—

> 3 cups sliced rhubarb (about 1 pound)
> 1 cup light corn syrup
> 2 tablespoons water
> ¼ cup orange liqueur *or* crème de cassis
> Few drops red food coloring (optional)

In a 2-quart nonmetal casserole combine the sliced rhubarb, light corn syrup, and water. In the *microwave oven* cook, covered, on high power for 4 to 6 minutes or till the rhubarb is tender, stirring once during cooking.

Pour the cooked rhubarb mixture into a blender container or food processor bowl. Cover and blend or process till the mixture is smooth. Add the orange liqueur or crème de cassis and a few drops red food coloring, if desired. Cover; blend or process till combined.

Pour the mixture into a 9x9x2-inch container; cover with moisture-vaporproof wrap or container lid. Chill in the *freezer* about 3 hours or till firm.

Break the frozen mixture into chunks and place in a chilled large mixer bowl. Beat on medium speed of electric mixer till smooth. Return the beaten mixture to the container and cover tightly. Chill in the *freezer* about 2 hours more or till firm. To serve, spoon the frozen mixture into dessert dishes. Makes about 1 quart (16 servings).

FROZEN ALMOND TARTS

¾ of an 8-ounce bar milk chocolate, broken up
2 tablespoons butter *or* margarine
20 marshmallows
⅓ cup milk
1 tablespoon instant coffee crystals
3 tablespoons Amaretto
½ cup whipping cream
  Whipped cream (optional)
  Sliced almonds (optional)

In a 2-cup glass measure place the chocolate and butter or margarine. In the *microwave oven* cook, uncovered, on high power about 1 minute or till soft. Stir just till combined. *Do not overstir.*

Place 8 paper bake cups in muffin pans. Spoon about *1 tablespoon* chocolate mixture into *each* bake cup; spread evenly with narrow metal spatula over bottom and up sides of bake cups. Chill in the *freezer* just till firm.

In a 2-quart nonmetal casserole combine the marshmallows, milk, and coffee crystals. In the *microwave oven* cook, uncovered, on high power for 2½ to 3 minutes or till marshmallows are melted, stirring twice during cooking. Stir in the Amaretto. Chill the mixture in the *freezer* for 30 to 45 minutes or till cold but not set, stirring twice.

In a mixing bowl beat the ½ cup whipping cream till soft peaks form (tips curl over). Gradually fold the marshmallow mixture into the whipped cream. Spoon the mixture into chocolate cups in muffin pans. Chill in the *freezer* at least 1 hour or till firm.

Before serving, remove the tarts from muffin pans. Peel the paper bake cups from chocolate tart shells. Top each tart with additional whipped cream and sliced almonds, if desired. Makes 8 servings.

FROZEN CRANBERRY TORTE

Pictured on page 66—

⅓ cup butter *or* margarine
1½ cups finely crushed graham crackers
½ cup finely chopped pecans
¼ cup sugar
1½ cups chopped cranberries (2 cups whole cranberries)
1 cup sugar
2 egg whites
1 tablespoon frozen orange juice concentrate
1 teaspoon vanilla
⅛ teaspoon salt
1 cup whipping cream
  Cranberry Topping

Place butter or margarine in a non-metal mixing bowl. In the *microwave oven* cook, uncovered, on high power for 1 to 1¼ minutes or till melted. Stir in the crushed graham crackers, pecans, and the ¼ cup sugar; press firmly against bottom and up sides of an 8-inch springform pan. Chill in the *freezer* till set.

Meanwhile, in a large mixing bowl combine the cranberries and the 1 cup sugar; let stand for 5 minutes. Add egg whites, orange juice concentrate, vanilla, and salt. Beat on low speed of electric mixer till frothy. Beat on high speed for 8 to 12 minutes or till stiff peaks form (tips stand straight). In a mixing bowl beat the cream till soft peaks form (tips curl over); fold into the cranberry mixture. Turn into crust. Chill in the *freezer* till firm.

Prepare Cranberry Topping. Before serving, remove sides of springform pan. Transfer torte to plate. Spoon Cranberry Topping atop. Serve immediately. Makes 8 to 10 servings.

Cranberry Topping: In 4-cup glass measure stir together ½ cup *sugar* and 1 tablespoon *cornstarch*; stir in ¾ cup chopped *cranberries* and ⅓ cup *water*.

In the *microwave oven* cook, uncovered, on high power for 2 to 4 minutes or till thickened and bubbly, stirring after every minute. Cool thoroughly.

HOT BUTTERED RUM MIX

Pictured on pages 4 and 5—

1 cup butter *or* margarine, softened
½ cup sifted powdered sugar
½ cup packed brown sugar
1 teaspoon ground nutmeg
1 teaspoon ground cinnamon
1 pint vanilla ice cream
4½ cups rum *or* brandy
12 cinnamon sticks (optional)

In a mixing bowl combine the butter or margarine, powdered sugar, brown sugar, nutmeg, and cinnamon. Beat on high speed of electric mixer till fluffy.

In a chilled mixing bowl stir the vanilla ice cream just to soften. Fold softened ice cream into the sugar mixture. Turn the mixture into a 4-cup moisture-vaporproof container. Seal tightly and label. Chill in the *freezer* till ready to use (mixture will not freeze solid).

To serve, spoon ¼ cup of the ice cream mixture into a 6- or 10-ounce nonmetal mug. Stir in *3 tablespoons* of the rum or brandy and ½ or ¾ cup *water*, depending on size of mug. Repeat with enough remaining ice cream mixture, rum or brandy, and water to make desired number of servings (up to 12 servings). Return any unused ice cream mixture to the *freezer* till ready to use.

In the *microwave oven* cook, uncovered, on high power till ice cream mixture is melted and liquid is hot. Allow 30 to 45 seconds for one 6-ounce mug, 1½ to 2 minutes for two 6-ounce mugs, 1 to 1¼ minutes for one 10-ounce mug, or 2 to 2¼ minutes for two 10-ounce mugs. Stir before serving. Garnish each serving with a cinnamon stick, if desired. Makes 12 servings.

microwave-plus menus

When you're preparing several foods for a meal or party, let your microwave oven step in to help. The following menus offer a sampling of breakfasts, brunches, lunches, and dinners. We've even included a picnic and a cocktail party that you can make several hours or a day ahead. The recipes use either the microwave oven or another major kitchen appliance, or a combination of both in order to provide you with the most efficient meal preparation schedule possible.

To guide you in scheduling your menu preparation, we've

suited to the job. By allowing each appliance to perform the tasks it does best, you create the most appealing foods possible in the shortest time and with the least effort.

With this book, you will learn to use your microwave oven and your other major appliances to their fullest potential to create individual recipes as well as entire menus. For example, precook a pizza crust in your conventional oven to make it crisp while quickly making the sauce in the microwave oven. Then assemble the pizza and pop it back into

the conventional oven to finish cooking.

The recipes pictured above represent uses of the microwave oven with various appliances and are from the various appliance chapters: Crispy Mandarin Pork from the rangetop chapter, Vegetable-Ham Roll from the oven chapter, Cornish Hens with Pepperoni Stuffing from the grill chapter, Corned Beef and Cabbage Molds from the refrigerator chapter, and Hot Buttered Rum Mix from the freezer chapter. (See Index for recipe pages.)

BREAKFAST MENU

Beer Pancakes
with Sausage

Cranberry Applesauce

Coffee Nog

COFFEE NOG

⅓ cup powdered eggnog
2 tablespoons instant coffee
    crystals
3½ cups milk
    Ground nutmeg

15 MINUTES BEFORE SERVING

In a 4-cup glass measure combine the powdered eggnog and coffee crystals. Stir in milk.

In the *microwave oven* cook, uncovered, on high power for 6 to 7 minutes or till dry ingredients are dissolved and mixture is heated through, stirring once during cooking. Pour into four 8-ounce coffee mugs. Sprinkle each serving with nutmeg. Makes 4 servings.

BEER PANCAKES WITH SAUSAGE

2 cups packaged biscuit mix
2 tablespoons sugar
½ teaspoon ground cinnamon
    Dash ground nutmeg
5 beaten eggs
½ cup beer
2 tablespoons cooking oil
8 fresh pork sausage links
1 cup pure maple syrup *or*
    maple-flavored syrup
    Butter *or* margarine

40 MINUTES BEFORE SERVING

In a large mixing bowl stir together the packaged biscuit mix, sugar, ground cinnamon, and ground nutmeg. In another mixing bowl combine the beaten eggs, beer, and cooking oil; add all at once to dry ingredients, stirring just till blended but still slightly lumpy. Stir in additional beer, if thinner pancakes are desired.

20 MINUTES BEFORE SERVING

Lightly grease a griddle or heavy skillet; heat on the *range top*. Pour ¼ cup batter for each pancake onto the hot griddle. Cook pancakes, a few at a time, on one side about 2 minutes or till pancakes have a bubbly surface and slightly dry edges. Turn and cook about 2 minutes more or till brown on both sides.

Meanwhile, on the *range top*, in a skillet cook the sausage links over medium heat for 8 to 10 minutes or till done. Remove and drain on paper toweling.

5 MINUTES BEFORE SERVING

Pour syrup into a 2-cup glass measure or small nonmetal pitcher. In the *microwave oven* cook, uncovered, on high power about 1½ minutes or till warm.

Serve pancakes and sausage with butter or margarine and maple syrup. Makes 10 to 12 (4-inch) pancakes.

Note: To reheat, cover pancakes with waxed paper. In the *microwave oven* cook pancakes, 3 at a time, on high power for 40 to 45 seconds or till heated through.

CRANBERRY APPLESAUCE

You can use either apples or pears, or a combination of both in this rose-colored applesauce—

2 medium apples *or* pears *or*
    1 medium apple *and* 1 medium
    pear
1 8-ounce can (1 cup) whole
    cranberry sauce
    Granola

50 MINUTES BEFORE SERVING

Cut the 2 apples or pears or the 1 apple and 1 pear into quarters. Core *each* of the quarters and peel; discard the peel and cores. Chop the fruit. In a 1½-quart nonmetal casserole stir together chopped apple and/or pear and whole cranberry sauce.

30 MINUTES BEFORE SERVING

In the *microwave oven* cook the fruit, covered, on high power for 8 to 10 minutes or till tender. If a smooth applesauce is desired, mash the cooked fruit with a potato masher till smooth. (*Or,* mash slightly for chunky applesauce.)

Serve applesauce warm or chilled. To chill, place the applesauce in the *refrigerator* about 20 minutes or till serving time. Sprinkle each serving with granola. Makes 4 servings.

Beer Pancakes with Sausage

BRUNCH MENU

Grapes in Grapefruit

Ham and Egg Casserole

Raisin Coffee Cake

Coffee or Tea

GRAPES IN GRAPEFRUIT

3 medium grapefruit, halved
1 8-ounce can pineapple tidbits, drained
⅔ cup seedless green grapes, halved
¼ cup maraschino cherries, halved
1 tablespoon butter *or* margarine
½ cup coconut
⅓ cup packed brown sugar

75 MINUTES BEFORE SERVING

Remove fruit from grapefruit halves, leaving shells intact. Cut fruit into chunks. Discard seeds and membranes. Combine grapefruit chunks, pineapple, grapes, and cherries; spoon into the grapefruit shells. Cover and chill in the *refrigerator.*

10 MINUTES BEFORE SERVING

Place filled grapefruit shells in the *microwave oven.* Cook, loosely covered, on high power for 4 minutes, rearranging once. In a nonmetal mixing bowl micro-cook butter or margarine, uncovered, on high for 30 seconds. Stir in coconut and brown sugar; spoon over fruit. Place on rack of unheated *broiler* pan; broil 3 inches from heat for 2 to 3 minutes or till bubbly. Makes 6 servings.

RAISIN COFFEE CAKE

1 cup water
½ cup raisins
2 cups all-purpose flour
½ cup sugar
1 tablespoon baking powder
½ teapoon salt
½ teaspoon ground cardamom
½ cup shortening
¾ cup milk
2 tablespoons butter *or* margarine
¼ cup packed brown sugar
¼ cup chopped pecans

2 HOURS BEFORE SERVING

In the *microwave oven* cook water in a nonmetal mixing bowl, uncovered, on high power for 1½ to 2 minutes or till boiling. Add raisins; let stand for 5 minutes. Drain well.

For dough, in a mixing bowl stir together the flour, sugar, baking powder, salt, and cardamom. Cut in shortening till mixture resembles coarse crumbs. Make a well in the center of the dry mixture; add milk all at once. Stir with a fork just till the dough clings together.

Turn the dough out onto a lightly floured surface; knead gently for 10 to 12 strokes. Reserve ¼ of the dough; pat the remaining dough against bottom and up sides of a greased 8x1½-inch round baking dish.

For filling, in a nonmetal mixing bowl micro-cook the butter or margarine, uncovered, on high about 30 seconds or till melted. Stir in the raisins, brown sugar, and chopped pecans; turn into the dough-lined baking dish.

On a lightly floured surface, roll the reserved dough to ¼-inch thickness. Cut into ½-inch-wide strips. Weave strips across the filling to make a lattice top.

1 HOUR BEFORE SERVING

Bake the coffee cake in the conventional oven at 375° for 25 to 30 minutes or till a wooden pick inserted near the center comes out clean. Cool before serving. Makes 1 coffee cake.

HAM AND EGG CASSEROLE

8 eggs
¼ cup sliced green onion
3 tablespoons butter *or* margarine
¼ cup all-purpose flour
⅛ teaspoon pepper
1½ cups milk
½ cup shredded process Swiss cheese (2 ounces)
1½ cups cubed fully cooked ham (8 ounces)
¼ cup coarsely crushed rich round crackers
1 tablespoon snipped parsley
1 tablespoon butter *or* margarine, melted

1 HOUR BEFORE SERVING

To hard-cook eggs, place eggs in a saucepan on the *range top;* cover with cold water. Bring to boiling; reduce heat to just below simmering. Cover and cook for 15 minutes. Run cold water over eggs till cool. Remove shells and slice eggs.

Meanwhile, for sauce, in a 4-cup glass measure combine green onion and the 3 tablespoons butter or margarine; cover with vented clear plastic wrap. In the *microwave oven* cook on high power for 1 to 2 minutes or till the green onion is tender.

Stir in the flour and pepper; add milk. Micro-cook, uncovered, on high for 4 to 5 minutes or till thickened and bubbly, stirring after every minute. Add shredded cheese, stirring till melted.

In the bottom of an 8x1½-inch round baking dish, arrange *half* of the hard-cooked egg slices; top with *half* of the ham and *half* of the sauce. Repeat layers.

For topping, combine the crushed crackers, parsley, and the 1 tablespoon melted butter or margarine; sprinkle atop casserole.

30 MINUTES BEFORE SERVING

Bake the casserole in the *conventional oven* at 350° about 25 minutes or till heated through. Makes 6 servings.

LUNCH MENU

Chicken-Stuffed Spuds

Aniseed Vegetable
Vinaigrette

Hot Mocha Sundaes

Beverage

HOT MOCHA SUNDAES

Vanilla ice cream
¼ **cup semisweet chocolate pieces**
2 **tablespoons light corn syrup**
1 **tablespoon milk**
1 **teaspoon instant coffee crystals**
Chopped pistachio nuts *or*
walnuts

35 MINUTES BEFORE SERVING

Scoop the vanilla ice cream into 2 dessert dishes; store in the *freezer* till serving time.

5 MINUTES BEFORE SERVING

For chocolate sauce, in the *microwave oven* cook the semisweet chocolate pieces in a small nonmetal bowl, covered, on high power about 1 minute or till the chocolate is melted, stirring once during cooking.

Stir in the corn syrup, milk, and coffee crystals; micro-cook, uncovered, on high about 30 seconds more or till heated through.

Top the ice cream with the chocolate sauce; sprinkle each serving with pistachio nuts or walnuts. Makes 2 servings.

ANISEED VEGETABLE VINAIGRETTE

2 **asparagus spears, cut in half**
crosswise
1 **stalk celery, cut into 2-inch strips**
1 **medium carrot, cut into 2-inch**
strips
2 **tablespoons water**
¼ **cup salad oil**
3 **tablespoons vinegar**
2 **teaspoons sugar**
¼ **teaspoon salt**
⅛ **teaspoon aniseed, crushed**
⅛ **teaspoon pepper**
Lettuce leaves (optional)

2 HOURS BEFORE SERVING

Place the asparagus, celery strips, carrot strips, and the water in a 10x6x2-inch nonmetal baking dish; cover tightly with vented clear plastic wrap. In the *microwave oven* cook on high power for 3 minutes, giving dish a half-turn once during cooking. Let stand, covered, about 3 minutes or till carrots are crisp-tender. Drain.

For dressing, in a screw-top jar combine salad oil, vinegar, sugar, salt, aniseed, and pepper. Cover the jar tightly and shake well to mix.

Pour the dressing over the vegetables in baking dish. Cover and chill in the *refrigerator* for at least 1½ hours or till serving time. (*Or,* prepare ahead and chill up to 24 hours.)

10 MINUTES BEFORE SERVING

To serve, lift vegetables from dressing with a slotted spoon. Arrange the vegetables on lettuce-lined salad plates, if desired. Spoon some of the dressing over vegetables. Pass the remaining dressing. Makes 2 servings.

CHICKEN-STUFFED SPUDS

2 **large baking potatoes (about 1**
pound)
¼ **cup chopped green pepper**
2 **tablespoons snipped chives**
2 **tablespoons butter *or* margarine**
1½ **cups chopped cooked chicken *or***
turkey
½ **cup cream-style cottage cheese**
¼ **teaspoon salt**
⅛ **teaspoon ground savory**
⅛ **teaspoon pepper**

30 MINUTES BEFORE SERVING

Wash, prick, and place the potatoes on paper toweling in the *microwave oven.* Cook, uncovered, on high power for 8 to 10 minutes, rearranging potatoes once during cooking. Let stand for 5 minutes or till cool enough to handle.

Meanwhile, in a 1-cup glass measure combine green pepper, chives, and butter or margarine; cover with vented clear plastic wrap. Micro-cook on high about 1 minute or till the green pepper is tender.

15 MINUTES BEFORE SERVING

Cut a lengthwise slice from the top of each potato; remove and discard skin from slice. Reserving potato shells, scoop out the insides and add to potato portions from top slices; mash.

For stuffing, use *only* about ¼ cup of the mashed potato. (Reserve remaining mashed potato for later.) In a mixing bowl combine the ¼ cup mashed potato, the green pepper mixture, chicken or turkey, *undrained* cottage cheese, salt, savory, and pepper.

Spoon the potato stuffing into the potato shells. Place in a 10x6x2-inch nonmetal baking dish; micro-cook, uncovered, on high for 2 to 3 minutes or till heated through. Makes 2 servings.

LUNCH MENU

Scallop Pasta Salad

Swiss Brioche

Cinnamon Poached
Peaches

Iced Tea

CINNAMON POACHED PEACHES

- 4 **small peaches** *or* **apples, peeled, halved, and pitted** *or* **cored**
- ¾ **cup apple juice**
- 1 **tablespoon honey**
- 3 **inches stick cinnamon**
- ¼ **teaspoon vanilla**
- 2 **medium kiwi, peeled and sliced**
  Ground cinnamon

30 MINUTES BEFORE SERVING

In a 2-quart nonmetal casserole combine the peach or apple halves, apple juice, honey, stick cinnamon, and vanilla. In the *microwave oven* cook, covered, on high power for 1 to 4 minutes or till fruit is tender, giving dish a half-turn once during cooking and spooning juice over fruit.

Transfer fruit to 4 dessert dishes. Arrange kiwi slices around fruit. Remove stick cinnamon from juice; pour juice over the fruit. Sprinkle ground cinnamon atop. Serve warm or chill in the *refrigerator* till serving time. Makes 4 servings.

Scallop Pasta Salad, Cinnamon Poached Peaches, and Swiss Brioche

SCALLOP PASTA SALAD

For added appeal, arrange the salad ingredients on spinach-lined salad plates—

- 8 **ounces fresh** *or* **frozen scallops**
- ¼ **cup water**
- ⅛ **teaspoon salt**
- 4 **ounces linguine** *or* **spaghetti, broken**
- 1 **11-ounce can mandarin orange sections, drained**
- 2 **tablespoons finely chopped green onion**
- ¼ **cup white wine vinegar**
- 2 **tablespoons salad oil**
- 1 **teaspoon finely shredded orange peel**
- ¾ **teaspoon dry mustard**
  Dash ground red pepper
- 1 **6-ounce package frozen pea pods, thawed**
  Spinach leaves (optional)
- ¼ **cup slivered almonds, toasted**

4 HOURS BEFORE SERVING

If frozen, let scallops stand at room temperature for 20 minutes. Halve any large scallops. In a 2-quart nonmetal casserole combine the scallops, water, and salt. In the *microwave oven* cook, covered, on high power for 3 to 5 minutes or till scallops are opaque, stirring once during cooking. Drain, cool, and slice.

Meanwhile, on the *range top* cook linguine or spaghetti according to package directions. Drain and cool. Combine the scallops, pasta, orange sections, and green onion.

For dressing, in a screw-top jar combine vinegar, oil, orange peel, dry mustard, and red pepper. Cover; shake well.

Pour dressing over scallop mixture. Toss gently to coat. Cover; chill in the *refrigerator* for 3½ hours. (*Or,* prepare ahead and chill up to 24 hours.)

5 MINUTES BEFORE SERVING

Stir pea pods into pasta mixture. Serve in a spinach-lined salad bowl, if desired. Sprinkle with slivered almonds. Makes 4 servings.

SWISS BRIOCHE

- 1 **package active dry yeast**
- ¼ **cup butter** *or* **margarine**
- 3 **tablespoons sugar**
- ¼ **teaspoon salt**
- 2 **cups all-purpose flour**
- ¼ **cup milk**
- 2 **eggs**
- ¼ **teaspoon ground nutmeg**
- ¼ **cup finely shredded Swiss cheese**
  Butter *or* **margarine, melted**

4 HOURS BEFORE SERVING

Soften yeast in 2 tablespoons warm *water* (110° to 115°). Cream the ¼ cup butter or margarine, sugar, and salt till fluffy. Add *½ cup* of the flour, the milk, eggs, and nutmeg to creamed mixture. Add the softened yeast; beat well. Stir in the remaining flour till smooth. Turn dough into a lightly greased nonmetal bowl; turn once to grease the surface.

Cover dough; let rise in a warm place till double (about 2 hours). (*Or,* let dough rise in the *microwave oven* for 7 to 10 minutes, following tip on page 41.) Punch dough down. Cover; let rest for 10 minutes.

On a lightly floured surface divide dough into three portions; set one portion aside. Divide *each* remaining portion into 4 pieces, making a total of 8. Form each piece into a large ball. Place each large ball in a greased 6-ounce nonmetal custard cup. Divide reserved dough into 8 pieces; shape into small balls.

Make an indention in each large ball. Press in about *1½ teaspoons* of the Swiss cheese. Press a small ball of dough into each. Brush melted butter or margarine over dough.

Cover; let rise in a warm place till nearly double (40 to 45 minutes). (*Or,* let dough rise, uncovered, in the *microwave oven* for 6 to 8 minutes or till nearly double, following tip on page 41.)

20 MINUTES BEFORE SERVING

Bake in the *conventional oven* at 375° for 10 to 15 minutes or till done. Serve warm. Makes 8 rolls.

PICNIC MENU

Barbecued Pork
Sandwiches

Two-Bean Slaw

Dilled Macaroni Salad

Sunshine Apple Mold

Pineapple Cake

Lemon-Lime Cooler

LEMON-LIME COOLER

- 1 6-ounce can frozen lemonade concentrate, thawed
- 1 6-ounce can frozen limeade concentrate, thawed
- 1 32-ounce bottle carbonated water
- ½ cup gin, vodka, *or* orange juice Ice cubes
  Lemon *or* lime slices (optional)

5 MINUTES BEFORE SERVING

In a large pitcher combine the lemonade and limeade concentrates. Stir in the carbonated water and the gin, vodka, or orange juice. Serve over ice cubes in tall glasses. Garnish each serving with lemon or lime slices, if desired. Makes 10 (5-ounce) servings.

BARBECUED PORK SANDWICHES

Hickory chips (1½ to 2 pounds)
Easy Barbecue Sauce
2 5-pound pork shoulder blade Boston roasts
1 tablespoon cornstarch
10 hard rolls *or* individual French rolls

7 HOURS BEFORE SERVING

Soak hickory chips in enough water to cover. Prepare Easy Barbecue Sauce.

6 HOURS BEFORE SERVING

In the covered *barbecue grill* arrange *medium-slow* coals around a heavy foil drip pan. Drain *some* of the hickory chips. Sprinkle atop coals. Trim excess fat from pork roasts. Place roasts, skin side up, on the grill above drip pan. Insert a meat thermometer near center of each roast, not touching fat or bone. Brush with *some* of the Easy Barbecue Sauce. Lower grill hood. Grill for 3 hours, adding coals and drained hickory chips as necessary and brushing with the barbecue sauce occasionally.

Turn roasts; brush with additional barbecue sauce. Lower grill hood; grill for 2 to 2½ hours more or till meat thermometers register 170° (meat should be very well done and should shred easily). Add coals and hickory chips as necessary and brush often with the barbecue sauce. (Use about *half* of the sauce to brush on meat while cooking.)

30 MINUTES BEFORE SERVING

Remove the pork roasts from grill. Cool slightly. Shred meat using two forks.

On the *range top*, in a saucepan combine remaining barbecue sauce (you should have about 2 cups) and cornstarch. Cook and stir till thickened and bubbly. Cook and stir for 2 minutes more. Serve shredded meat on rolls; pass the sauce. Makes 10 to 12 servings.

Easy Barbecue Sauce: In a 1½-quart nonmetal casserole stir together 1 cup packed *brown sugar*, 1½ teaspoons onion salt, ½ teaspoon *salt*, ½ teaspoon *paprika*, ½ teapoon *pepper*, and dash *garlic salt*. Stir in 2 cups *vinegar*, 1 cup *bottled barbecue sauce*, ½ cup *catsup*, 2 tablespoons *Worcestershire sauce*, and ½ to 1 teaspoon *bottled hot pepper sauce*. In the *microwave oven* cook, uncovered, on high power about 4 minutes or till sugar is dissolved.

SUNSHINE APPLE MOLD

- 2 cups apple cider *or* apple juice
- 2 3-ounce packages *or* one 6-ounce package lemon-flavored gelatin
- 1 3-ounce package cream cheese, softened
- 1½ cups cold water
- ¼ teaspoon ground ginger
- 2 medium oranges, peeled, sectioned, and cut up (¾ cup)
- 1 large apple, cored and chopped (1 cup)

24 HOURS BEFORE SERVING

In a nonmetal mixing bowl combine apple cider or juice and lemon-flavored gelatin. In the *microwave oven* cook, uncovered, on high power for 4 to 6 minutes or till gelatin is dissolved, stirring twice during cooking.

Add softened cream cheese to gelatin mixture; beat with a rotary beater till smooth. Stir in the cold water and ground ginger. Chill in the *refrigerator* till the mixture is the consistency of unbeaten egg whites (partially set).

Fold the orange sections and the chopped apple into gelatin mixture; turn into a 10x6x2-inch container. Chill in the *refrigerator* overnight or till firm.

25 MINUTES BEFORE SERVING

Cut the gelatin salad into squares to serve. Makes 10 servings.

TWO-BEAN SLAW

- 1 tablespoon butter *or* margarine
- 2 tablespoons sugar
- 4 teaspoons all-purpose flour
- 1 teaspoon dry mustard
- 1 teaspoon caraway seed
- ½ teaspoon salt
  Dash white pepper
- ¾ cup milk
- 1 8-ounce carton plain yogurt
- 1 9-ounce package frozen cut green beans
- 2 tablespoons water
- 3 cups shredded cabbage
- 1 15½-ounce can red kidney beans, drained
- 1 cup chopped cucumber
- ½ cup chopped celery
- ½ cup shredded carrot
- ½ cup chopped green pepper

24 HOURS BEFORE SERVING

For dressing, in a 4-cup glass measure place butter or margarine. In a *microwave oven* cook, uncovered, on high power about 30 seconds or till melted. Stir in sugar, flour, dry mustard, caraway seed, salt, and white pepper. Add milk. Micro-cook, uncovered, on high for 2 to 4 minutes or till thickened and bubbly, stirring after every 30 seconds. Micro-cook, uncovered, on high for 1 minute more, stirring once. Stir in the yogurt. Cover and chill in the *refrigerator* overnight.

Place the frozen green beans and the water in a 1-quart nonmetal casserole. In a *microwave oven* cook, covered, on high power for 4 to 7 minutes, stirring once during cooking. Let stand, covered, for 3 minutes. Drain.

In a large bowl or container combine the cooked green beans, the cabbage, kidney beans, cucumber, celery, carrot, and green pepper. Cover and chill in the *refrigerator* overnight.

20 MINUTES BEFORE SERVING

Pour the chilled dressing over vegetables; toss gently to coat. Season to taste with salt and pepper. Makes 10 servings.

DILLED MACARONI SALAD

- 1½ cups elbow macaroni
- 1½ cups frozen peas
- 2 tablespoons water
- 6 slices bacon
- 1 cup cubed American cheese
- 1 cup sliced fresh mushrooms
- ¾ cup mayonnaise *or* salad dressing
- 3 tablespoons vinegar
- 1 teaspoon salt
- 1 teaspoon dried dillweed
- 1 cup cherry tomatoes, halved

24 HOURS BEFORE SERVING

On the *range top* cook the macaroni in boiling, salted water according to package directions; drain and cool.

Meanwhile, in a 2-cup glass measure combine the frozen peas and water; cover with vented clear plastic wrap. In the *microwave oven* cook on high power for 3 to 5 minutes or till tender, stirring once during cooking. Let stand for 3 minutes; drain well and set aside.

Place the bacon between paper toweling on a paper plate. Micro-cook on high about 5 minutes or till crisp. Crumble and set aside.

In a large bowl or container combine cooked macaroni, peas, bacon pieces, cheese cubes, and mushroom slices.

For dressing, stir together the mayonnaise or salad dressing, vinegar, salt, and dillweed; add to macaroni mixture. Toss gently to coat. Cover and chill in the *refrigerator* overnight.

15 MINUTES BEFORE SERVING

Add the cherry tomato halves and toss gently. Makes 10 servings.

PINEAPPLE CAKE

- 2 cups sugar
- 1 cup shortening
- 1 teaspoon vanilla
- 4 egg yolks
- 3 cups self-rising flour
- 1½ cups milk
- 4 stiff-beaten egg whites
- 2 20-ounce cans crushed pineapple
- ⅔ cup sugar
- 2 tablespoons butter *or* margarine
- 1 cup whipping cream
- 2 tablespoons sugar

5 HOURS BEFORE SERVING

Grease and lightly flour three 9x1½-inch round baking pans. Beat the 2 cups sugar, shortening, and vanilla with electric mixer till fluffy. Add egg yolks, one at a time, beating about 1 minute after each addition. Add flour and milk alternately to beaten mixture, beating after each addition. Fold in beaten egg whites. Pour into pans. Bake in the *conventional oven* at 350° about 25 minutes or till done. Cool for 10 minutes on wire racks. Remove from pans; cool thoroughly.

Meanwhile, drain pineapple well, reserving ⅔ cup of the syrup. In a 4-cup glass measure combine reserved syrup, the ⅔ cup sugar, and the butter or margarine. In the *microwave oven* cook, uncovered, on high power about 3 minutes or till sugar is dissolved. Prick top of cake layers with fork. Carefully spoon ⅓ cup of the syrup mixture over *each* cake layer.

For filling, stir drained pineapple into remaining syrup mixture; micro-cook, uncovered, on high about 2 minutes or till heated through. Stack the cake layers, spooning ¾ cup of the filling between *each* layer. Spoon remaining filling over top of cake. Chill in the *refrigerator* about 2 hours or till serving time.

10 MINUTES BEFORE SERVING

Whip cream and the 2 tablespoons sugar till soft peaks form. Dollop atop each serving of cake. Pass remaining whipped cream. Serves 12 to 16.

COCKTAIL PARTY MENU

Pictured on pages 74 and 75

Pork Egg Rolls

Mustard-Glazed Meatballs

Orange-Coconut Dip with Fruit Dippers

Creole-Style Party Mix

Sparkling Lime and Ginger Tea

Rosé Cooler

ROSÉ COOLER

    2 cups orange juice
    ⅓ cup honey
    2 750-milliliter bottles rosé wine
    1 28-ounce bottle carbonated
        water, chilled
      Ice cubes

24 HOURS BEFORE SERVING

Combine juice and honey. In the *microwave oven* cook, uncovered, on high power for 1 to 2 minutes. Cool; stir into wine. Cover and chill in the *refrigerator*.

10 MINUTES BEFORE SERVING

Slowly stir carbonated water into wine mixture. Serve over ice cubes in glasses. Garnish with orange wedges and maraschino cherries, if desired. Makes about 20 (5-ounce) servings.

MUSTARD-GLAZED MEATBALLS

    1 beaten egg
    ¼ cup fine dry bread crumbs
    ½ pound lean ground beef
    ½ cup finely chopped cooked
        corned beef
    ½ cup apple juice *or* apple cider
    2 teaspoons cornstarch
    1 teaspoon prepared mustard
    ½ teaspoon instant beef bouillon
        granules
    1 tablespoon snipped parsley
      Snipped parsley (optional)

24 HOURS BEFORE SERVING

In a mixing bowl combine the beaten egg and bread crumbs. Add the ground beef and corned beef; mix well. Shape the mixture into ¾-inch meatballs. Place the meatballs in a shallow baking pan. Cover and chill in the *refrigerator*.

20 MINUTES BEFORE SERVING

Bake the meatballs in the *conventional oven* at 350° about 15 minutes or till done. Transfer to a serving bowl or chafing dish.

Meanwhile, for glaze, in a 2-cup glass measure combine apple juice or apple cider, cornstarch, mustard, and bouillon granules. In the *microwave oven* cook, uncovered, on high power for 2 to 3 minutes or till thickened and bubbly, stirring after every 30 seconds. Stir in the 1 tablespoon snipped parsley. Micro-cook, uncovered, on high about 30 seconds more.

To serve, pour the glaze over the meatballs in bowl or chafing dish. If desired, sprinkle with additional parsley. Serve with wooden picks. Makes about 16 servings.

CREOLE-STYLE PARTY MIX

Creoles in southern Louisiana like highly seasoned food and often add a lot of red pepper, garlic, onion, parsley, and celery to their dishes—

    ⅓ cup butter *or* margarine
    1½ teaspoons dried parsley flakes
    ½ teaspoon celery salt
    ½ teaspoon dried thyme, crushed
    ½ teaspoon bottled hot pepper
        sauce
    ¼ teaspoon garlic powder
    ¼ teaspoon onion powder
    3 cups bite-size shredded rice
        squares
    1½ cups small twisted pretzels
    1½ cups chow mein noodles
    1½ cups pecan halves
    8 slices bacon

24 HOURS BEFORE SERVING

In a 2-cup glass measure combine butter or margarine, parsley flakes, celery salt, thyme, bottled hot pepper sauce, garlic powder, and onion powder. In the *microwave oven* cook, uncovered, on high power for 1 to 1½ minutes or till the butter or margarine is melted.

In a large nonmetal mixing bowl combine the shredded rice squares, pretzels, chow mein noodles, and pecan halves. Pour the butter mixture over the cereal mixture, stirring gently to coat.

Micro-cook, uncovered, on high for 6 to 8 minutes or till toasted, stirring after every 2 minutes. Cool. Store the mixture in airtight containers.

1 HOUR BEFORE SERVING

Place the bacon slices between paper toweling on a paper plate. Micro-cook on high for 6½ to 7½ minutes or till done; crumble. Stir the cooked bacon pieces into the toasted cereal mixture. Makes about 16 servings.

ORANGE-COCONUT DIP WITH FRUIT DIPPERS

½ **cup coconut**
1 **3-ounce package cream cheese**
2 **8-ounce cartons orange yogurt**
⅛ **teaspoon ground cinnamon**
⅛ **teaspoon ground cloves**
  Assorted fruit dippers*

24 HOURS BEFORE SERVING

To toast coconut, spread it in a 9-inch nonmetal pie plate. In the *microwave oven* cook, uncovered, on high power for 3 to 4 minutes or till golden. After 1½ minutes of micro-cooking, stir the coconut after every 30 seconds.

To soften cream cheese, place it in a nonmetal mixing bowl. Micro-cook, uncovered, on high for 30 seconds. Let stand for 3 minutes.

For dip, gradually stir ⅓ *cup* of the coconut, the orange yogurt, ground cinnamon, and cloves into the softened cream cheese; stir till combined. (Wrap the remaining coconut and store in the *refrigerator* for a garnish.) Spoon the dip into a small serving bowl. Cover and chill in the *refrigerator*.

45 MINUTES BEFORE SERVING

Cut the assorted fruit into pieces for dipping as desired; brush the cut edges with lemon juice to prevent browning. Sprinkle the orange dip with the remaining toasted coconut. Cover and chill the fruit dippers and dip in the *refrigerator* till serving time. Makes 2½ cups dip.

*Note: Choose from the following fresh fruit for fruit dippers: apples, bananas, pineapple, cherries, pears, nectarines, strawberries, honeydew melon, or cantaloupe.

PORK EGG ROLLS

Do not reheat the egg rolls in the microwave oven as they will become soggy—

¾ **pound ground pork**
2 **cups finely chopped cabbage**
½ **cup chopped fresh mushrooms**
¼ **cup shredded carrot**
1 **tablespoon cooking oil**
2 **tablespoons dry sherry**
2 **tablespoons soy sauce**
2 **teaspoons cornstarch**
8 *or* 9 **egg roll skins**
  Cooking oil for deep-fat frying
  Chinese Mustard

6 HOURS BEFORE SERVING

For filling, in a 1½-quart nonmetal casserole cook pork, covered, in the *microwave oven* on high power for 3 to 4 minutes or till no pink remains, stirring once. Remove pork; drain and set aside. In same casserole combine cabbage, mushrooms, carrot, and the 1 tablespoon cooking oil. Micro-cook, covered, on high for 2 to 3 minutes or till crisp-tender, stirring once. Combine sherry, soy sauce, and cornstarch; add to vegetable mixture. Micro-cook, uncovered, on high for 2 to 4 minutes or till thickened and bubbly, stirring after every minute. Stir in pork. Cool.

Cut egg roll skins in half diagonally. Place about *2 tablespoons* of the filling in the center of *each* triangle about ½ inch from edge of wide end. Fold side corners over filling. Roll up toward remaining corner. Moisten edges with water; seal.

On *range top* fry, a few at a time, in deep hot oil (365°) for 2 to 3 minutes or till golden. Drain on paper toweling. Cool. Cover; store in *refrigerator*.

10 MINUTES BEFORE SERVING

Place egg rolls on a baking sheet. Bake in the *conventional oven* at 350° for 8 to 10 minutes or till heated through. Prepare Chinese Mustard; serve with egg rolls. Makes 16 to 18 egg rolls.

Chinese Mustard: Combine ¼ cup *dry mustard*, ¼ cup *water*, 2 teaspoons *cooking oil*, and ½ teaspoon *salt*.

SPARKLING LIME AND GINGER TEA

Micro-cook the gingerroot to bring out the ginger flavor for this refreshing version of iced tea—

6 **cups water**
⅓ **cup instant tea powder**
½ **cup sugar**
½ **cup water**
1 **1½-inch piece gingerroot, peeled and sliced**
¼ **cup lime juice**
2 **cups carbonated water, chilled**
  Ice cubes
  Lime slices (optional)
  Lemon slices (optional)

24 HOURS BEFORE SERVING

In a pitcher stir the 6 cups water into the instant tea powder. In a 2-cup glass measure combine sugar, the ½ cup water, and gingerroot; cover tightly with vented clear plastic wrap.

In the *microwave oven* cook the gingerroot mixture on high power for 2 to 2½ minutes or till heated through. Stir the hot mixture into the tea in pitcher. Stir in the lime juice. Cover and chill the mixture in the *refrigerator*.

5 MINUTES BEFORE SERVING

Remove the slices of gingerroot from the chilled tea mixture. Slowly stir the chilled carbonated water into the mixture, using an up-and-down motion.

To serve, pour tea over ice cubes in tall glasses. Garnish each serving with a lime slice and a lemon slice, if desired. Makes about 15 (5-ounce) servings.

DINNER MENU

Horseradish Pot Roast

Mustard-Whole Wheat
Rolls

Strawberries and Snow

Beverage

HORSERADISH POT ROAST

- 1 3-pound beef chuck pot roast
- 2 tablespoons cooking oil
- 1 10½-ounce can condensed beef broth
- 3 tablespoons prepared horseradish
- 4 medium potatoes, peeled and quartered
- 4 medium carrots, cut into chunks
- 1 medium onion, cut into wedges
- 2 tablespoons cornstarch

3 HOURS BEFORE SERVING

On the *range top* brown meat in hot oil. Combine *1 cup* beef broth, horseradish, ¼ teaspoon *salt*, and ¼ teaspoon *pepper*; pour over meat. Cover; simmer for 1¼ hours. Add vegetables. Cover; simmer about 45 minutes more or till tender.

10 MINUTES BEFORE SERVING

Transfer meat and vegetables to platter. Skim fat from juices. In 4-cup glass measure add water to juices to equal 1¾ cups liquid. Combine the remaining broth and cornstarch; stir into juices. In the *microwave oven* cook, uncovered, on high power for 2 to 4 minutes or till bubbly, stirring every 30 seconds. Serve with roast. Serves 6.

STRAWBERRIES AND SNOW

- 4 cups sliced strawberries
- ¼ cup sugar
- 2½ cups water
- 1 6-ounce package strawberry-flavored gelatin
- 1 envelope unflavored gelatin
- ½ cup sugar
- 1 cup water
- 3 tablespoons brandy
- 2 tablespoons orange liqueur
- ½ cup whipping cream
  Sliced strawberries (optional)

24 HOURS BEFORE SERVING

In a mixing bowl combine the 4 cups sliced strawberries and the ¼ cup sugar; set aside.

In a 4-cup glass measure stir the 2½ cups water into the strawberry-flavored gelatin. In the *microwave oven* cook, uncovered, on high power about 6 minutes or till gelatin is dissolved, stirring several times during cooking. Chill in the *refrigerator* till the mixture is the consistency of unbeaten egg whites (partially set).

Fold the sweetened strawberries into the partially set strawberry gelatin; pour into a 12x7½x2-inch container. Chill in the *refrigerator* till almost firm.

Meanwhile, in a 2-cup glass measure combine the unflavored gelatin and the ½ cup sugar; stir in the 1 cup water. In the *microwave oven* cook, uncovered, on high power for 2½ to 3 minutes or till gelatin is dissolved, stirring twice during cooking. Cool slightly. Stir in the brandy and orange liqueur. Chill in the *refrigerator* till consistency of unbeaten egg whites (partially set).

Beat the whipping cream till soft peaks form; fold into partially set brandy mixture. Pour the brandy-cream mixture over the almost-firm strawberry mixture. Cover and chill in the *refrigerator*.

5 MINUTES BEFORE SERVING

Cut the dessert into squares. Garnish with some additional sliced strawberries, if desired. Makes 10 servings.

MUSTARD-WHOLE WHEAT ROLLS

- 1 to 1½ cups all-purpose flour
- 1 package active dry yeast
- ½ cup milk
- 2 tablespoons sugar
- 1 tablespoon shortening
- 1 tablespoon prepared mustard
- ½ teaspoon salt
- 1 egg
- 1 cup whole wheat flour
  Milk
- 1 teaspoon poppy seed

3 HOURS BEFORE SERVING

Combine *1 cup* of the all-purpose flour and yeast; set aside. In a 2-cup glass measure combine the ½ cup milk, sugar, shortening, mustard, and salt. In the *microwave oven* cook, uncovered, on high power for 30 to 45 seconds or till warm (115° to 120°). Add to flour mixture; add egg. Beat on low speed of electric mixer for ½ minute, scraping sides of bowl. Beat 3 minutes on high speed. Stir in whole wheat flour and as much remaining all-purpose flour as possible.

On a lightly floured surface, knead in enough of remaining all-purpose flour to make a moderately stiff dough that is smooth and elastic (6 to 8 minutes total). Shape into a ball. Place in a greased nonmetal bowl; turn once to grease surface. Cover; let rise in a warm place till double (about 1 hour). (Or, read instructions for raising yeast bread in the *microwave oven* on page 41. Let the dough rise, covered, in the *microwave oven* on 10% power (LOW) for 16 to 20 minutes or till double.)

Punch down. Cover; let rest 10 minutes. Shape into 12 rolls. Place in a greased 8x1½-inch nonmetal round baking dish. Cover; let rise in a warm place till double (45 to 60 minutes). (Or, place in *microwave oven* beside water. Let rise, covered, on 10% power (LOW) 6 to 8 minutes or till nearly double.)

30 MINUTES BEFORE SERVING

Brush with milk; sprinkle with poppy seed. Bake in the *conventional oven* at 375° for 15 to 18 minutes. Makes 12.

DINNER MENU

Crispy Pork Schnitzel

Duchess Mushroom Casserole

Hot Sauerkraut

Cottage Cheese Crepes

Beverage

CRISPY PORK SCHNITZEL

6 pork sirloin cutlets, cut ½ inch thick
¼ cup all-purpose flour
1 teaspoon seasoned salt
2 beaten eggs
¼ cup milk
¾ cup fine dry bread crumbs
1 teaspoon paprika
3 tablespoons shortening
Creamy Dill Sauce

40 MINUTES BEFORE SERVING

Pound pork to ¼- to ⅛-inch thickness. Cut slits around edges. Combine flour, salt, and ¼ teaspoon *pepper*. Combine eggs and milk. Combine crumbs and paprika. Dip meat into flour mixture, then egg mixture. Coat with crumb mixture.

10 MINUTES BEFORE SERVING

On the *range top* cook pork in shortening for 5 minutes on each side. Prepare Creamy Dill Sauce. Serves 6.

Creamy Dill Sauce: In a 2-cup glass measure mix ½ cup *dairy sour cream,* 2 tablespoons *all-purpose flour,* and ¼ teaspoon dried *dillweed.* Stir in ¾ cup *chicken broth.* In *microwave oven* cook, uncovered, on high power for 2½ to 3 minutes or till bubbly; stir often.

COTTAGE CHEESE CREPES

12 Basic Dessert Crepes (see recipe, page 27)
2 slightly beaten eggs
1½ cups cream-style cottage cheese, well drained and sieved
½ teaspoon vanilla
Dash ground cinnamon
⅓ cup strawberry preserves
Whipped cream (optional)
Strawberry preserves (optional)

90 MINUTES BEFORE SERVING

Prepare Basic Dessert Crepes according to directions on page 27. For filling, in a medium mixing bowl combine the beaten eggs, sieved cottage cheese, vanilla, and cinnamon.

To assemble the crepes, spoon *1 rounded tablespoon* of the filling in the center of the unbrowned side of *each* crepe. Using the ⅓ cup strawberry preserves, top with *1 rounded teaspoon* preserves. Overlap the sides of crepes atop filling, then overlap ends.

Place the filled crepes, seam side down, in a 12x7½x2-inch nonmetal baking dish. Cover the dish with vented clear plastic wrap and chill in the *refrigerator* till serving time.

AT DESSERT TIME

In the *microwave oven* cook the filled crepes, covered, on high power for 5 to 6 minutes or till heated through. Dollop each serving with some whipped cream and additional strawberry preserves, if desired. Makes 6 servings.

DUCHESS MUSHROOM CASSEROLE

3 medium baking potatoes, peeled and quartered
1 tablespoon water
3 tablespoons butter *or* margarine
½ teaspoon salt
Dash pepper
2 beaten eggs
¼ cup milk
3 cups sliced fresh mushrooms
½ cup chopped onion
1 tablespoon butter *or* margarine
2 tablespoons snipped parsley
¼ cup shredded cheddar cheese (1 ounce)

1 HOUR BEFORE SERVING

Place the potato quarters and the water in a 1-quart nonmetal casserole. In the *microwave oven* cook, covered, on high power about 8 minutes or till potatoes are tender. Drain.

50 MINUTES BEFORE SERVING

Turn the cooked potato into a large mixing bowl; mash with a potato masher or beat on low speed of electric mixer. Add the 3 tablespoons butter or margarine, the salt, and pepper. Add eggs and milk; mash or beat till light and fluffy.

Meanwhile, in the same 1-quart nonmetal casserole combine the mushrooms, onion, and the 1 tablespoon butter or margarine. Cover and micro-cook on high about 5 minutes or till vegetables are tender, stirring once during cooking. Stir in parsley.

Turn about *half* of the mashed potato mixture into a greased 1½-quart casserole. Top with the mushroom mixture. Spread remaining potato mixture atop.

20 MINUTES BEFORE SERVING

Bake the casserole in the *conventional oven* at 400° for 15 to 18 minutes or till heated through. Sprinkle the shredded cheddar cheese atop; bake about 2 minutes more or till cheese is melted. Makes 6 servings.

DINNER MENU

Polish Sausage and
Vegetable Paprikash

Dill Spinach Bisque

Orange-Spice Cake

Beverage

DILL SPINACH BISQUE

- 1 10-ounce package frozen chopped spinach
- 1 teaspoon instant chicken bouillon granules
- 1½ cups milk
- 1 8-ounce carton plain yogurt
- ⅛ teaspoon dried dillweed
- 6 large green peppers (optional)

3 HOURS BEFORE SERVING

In a 1½-quart nonmetal casserole combine spinach, bouillon granules, and 2 tablespoons *water*. In *microwave oven* cook, covered, on high power 6 minutes or till tender; stir once.

In a blender container or food processor bowl combine *half* of the spinach and *half* of the milk. Cover and blend or process till spinach is finely chopped. Add *half* of the yogurt, the dillweed, and ⅛ teaspoon *pepper*. Cover and blend 1 minute or till smooth. Set aside. Repeat with remaining. Chill in *refrigerator*.

Prepare green pepper shells, if using for containers. Cut tops off peppers; remove seeds and scallop edges; chill.

5 MINUTES BEFORE SERVING

Stir spinach mixture; spoon into pepper shells, if desired, or bowls. Pass additional yogurt, if desired. Serves 6.

POLISH SAUSAGE AND VEGETABLE PAPRIKASH

- 1 10-ounce package frozen lima beans
- ⅔ cup water
- ½ cup chopped onion
- 2 tablespoons paprika
- ½ teaspoon instant chicken bouillon granules
- ½ teaspoon dried basil, crushed
  Few drops bottled hot pepper sauce
- 1 pound fully cooked Polish sausage *or* bratwurst, bias-sliced into ½-inch-thick slices
- 3 small yellow summer squash *or* zucchini, cut into bite-size chunks
- 12 cherry tomatoes, halved, *or* 1 large tomato, cut into wedges
- 1 10-ounce package spaetzle *or* 3 cups tiny shell macaroni *or* bow ties
  Fresh basil (optional)

40 MINUTES BEFORE SERVING

In a 3-quart nonmetal casserole combine lima beans, the water, onion, paprika, chicken bouillon granules, dried basil, and hot pepper sauce. In the *microwave oven* cook, covered, on high power about 5 minutes or till lima beans are tender, stirring once during cooking. Do not drain.

Stir in Polish sausage or bratwurst and yellow squash or zucchini. Micro-cook, covered, on high for 8 to 10 minutes or till the vegetables are almost tender, stirring once during cooking. Stir in the tomato pieces; micro-cook, covered, on high about 1 minute more or till heated through.

Meanwhile, on the *range top* cook spaetzle, shell macaroni, or bow ties in a 3-quart saucepan in boiling salted water according to package directions; drain.

Serve the sausage mixture with the hot cooked spaetzle or macaroni. Garnish with fresh basil, if desired. Makes 6 to 8 servings.

ORANGE-SPICE CAKE

- ⅔ cup all-purpose flour
- ¼ cup sugar
- ¼ cup packed brown sugar
- ½ teaspoon baking powder
- ½ teaspoon ground cinnamon
- ¼ teaspoon salt
- ¼ teaspoon ground ginger
- ⅓ cup buttermilk
- ¼ cup shortening
- 1 egg
- ¼ cup sugar
- 1 tablespoon cornstarch
- ⅛ teaspoon salt
- 1 cup orange juice
- 2 tablespoons butter *or* margarine
- ½ teaspoon vanilla

1 HOUR BEFORE SERVING

Grease and lightly flour a 7½x3½x2-inch loaf pan. Stir together flour, ¼ cup sugar, brown sugar, baking powder, cinnamon, ¼ teaspoon salt, and ginger. Add *half* of the buttermilk, shortening, and egg. Beat with electric mixer till moistened. Beat for 2 minutes more, scraping sides of bowl. Add remaining buttermilk; beat 1 minute more or till combined. Turn into prepared pan. Bake in the *conventional oven* at 350° for 30 to 35 minutes or till done. Cool on a wire rack.

15 MINUTES BEFORE SERVING

In a 4-cup glass measure combine ¼ cup sugar, cornstarch, and ⅛ teaspoon salt. Stir in orange juice. In the *microwave oven* cook, uncovered, on high power for 2 to 4 minutes or till thickened and bubbly, stirring after every 30 seconds. Stir in butter or margarine and the vanilla.

Remove cake from pan; cut into wedges. If desired, garnish with orange slice quarters. Spoon the warm sauce over each serving. Makes 8 servings.

Polish Sausage and Vegetable Paprikash, Dill Spinach Bisque, and Orange-Spice Cake

DINNER MENU

Cornish Hens à l'Orange

Wild Rice with Zucchini

Chocolate-Filled Pastry Alaskas

Coffee or Tea

CHOCOLATE-FILLED PASTRY ALASKAS

- 1 10-ounce package (6) frozen patty shells
- 3 cups chocolate ice cream
- ½ cup chopped pecans *or* walnuts
- 3 egg whites
- ½ teaspoon vanilla
- ¼ teaspoon cream of tartar
- ⅓ cup sugar

2 HOURS BEFORE SERVING

Place patty shells on a baking sheet; bake in the *conventional oven* according to package directions. Remove the soft centers and cool completely.

Working quickly, shape ice cream into 6 logs. Roll in nuts. Place one log in each patty shell. Store in the *freezer*.

AT DESSERT TIME

For meringue, beat egg whites, vanilla, and cream of tartar till soft peaks form. Gradually add the sugar, beating till stiff peaks form. Quickly coat the filled patty shells with meringue. Bake in the *conventional oven* at 500° about 2 minutes or till golden. Serve immediately. Makes 6 servings.

WILD RICE WITH ZUCCHINI

- 1 6-ounce package regular long grain and wild rice mix
- 2 tablespoons butter *or* margarine
- ½ teaspoon dried basil, crushed
- 3 medium zucchini *or* yellow summer squash, sliced (about 3 cups)
- ½ cup chopped fresh mushrooms
- ¼ cup water
- 1 7½-ounce can semi-condensed cream of mushroom soup
- ¾ cup dairy sour cream
  Snipped parsley (optional)

75 MINUTES BEFORE SERVING

On the *range top* cook the rice mix according to package directions. Stir in the butter or margarine and basil.

Meanwhile, in a 10x6x2-inch nonmetal baking dish combine the zucchini or yellow squash, mushrooms, and the water; cover tightly with vented clear plastic wrap. In the *microwave oven* cook on high power for 6 to 7 minutes or till squash is crisp-tender, stirring after 3 minutes. Remove from dish and drain well.

In a large mixing bowl combine the mushroom soup and sour cream. Stir the vegetable mixture into soup mixture.

Spread *half* of the rice mixture in the bottom of the 10x6x2-inch nonmetal baking dish. Spoon the vegetable mixture atop. Spread the remaining rice mixture atop the vegetable layer.

15 MINUTES BEFORE SERVING

Micro-cook the layered casserole, uncovered, on high about 8 minutes or till heated through, giving the dish a half-turn after 4 minutes. Sprinkle with fresh parsley, if desired. Makes 6 servings.

CORNISH HENS À L'ORANGE

- 3 1- to 1½-pound Cornish game hens, halved lengthwise
- ½ cup water
- ¼ cup orange peel cut into julienne strips
- 3 tablespoons brown sugar
- 2 tablespoons cornstarch
- ⅔ cup water
- ½ cup orange juice
- ½ teaspoon instant chicken bouillon granules
- ¼ teaspoon salt
- 1 tablespoon brandy
  Paprika (optional)

1 HOUR BEFORE SERVING

Rinse hens and pat dry. Sprinkle with salt and pepper. Place each poultry half, cut side down, on a large nonmetal platter. Cover with waxed paper. In the *microwave oven* cook on high power for 15 minutes. Rearrange birds. Micro-cook, covered, on high about 10 minutes more or till legs can be twisted easily in sockets. Let birds stand, covered, about 10 minutes.

In a small nonmetal bowl combine the ½ cup water and the orange peel strips. Micro-cook, uncovered, on high for 5 minutes. Drain and set orange peel strips aside.

10 MINUTES BEFORE SERVING

For sauce, on the *range top* combine the brown sugar and cornstarch in a saucepan. Stir in the ⅔ cup water, the orange juice, bouillon granules, and salt. Cook and stir over medium heat till thickened and bubbly. Cook and stir for 2 minutes more. Remove from heat. Stir in the orange peel strips and brandy.

To serve, sprinkle hens with paprika, if desired. Transfer hens to serving plates. Spoon some of the sauce atop each serving. Pass remaining sauce. Makes 6 servings.

DINNER MENU

Halibut with Sherry Sauce

Herb Rolls

Pistachio-Chocolate Parfaits

Beverage

HERB ROLLS

2 tablespoons butter *or* margarine
⅛ teaspoon dried thyme, crushed
⅛ teaspoon dried dillweed
1 package (8) refrigerated Parkerhouse rolls

45 MINUTES BEFORE SERVING

For herb butter, in a 6-ounce nonmetal custard cup combine the butter or margarine, dried thyme, and dillweed. In the *microwave oven* cook, uncovered, on high power about 30 seconds or till the butter or margarine is melted.

Place the unbaked rolls on an ungreased baking sheet. Brush the tops of the rolls with the herb butter instead of the melted butter called for in the package directions. Set aside.

15 MINUTES BEFORE SERVING

Bake the rolls in the *conventional oven* according to package directions. Serve warm. Makes 8 rolls.

PISTACHIO-CHOCOLATE PARFAITS

You can chill the pudding and sauce overnight and assemble the parfaits several hours before serving—

1 package 4-serving-size *instant* pistachio *or* vanilla pudding mix
1¾ cups milk
⅓ cup milk chocolate pieces
⅓ cup evaporated milk
2 tablespoons chopped almonds, walnuts, *or* peanuts

4 HOURS BEFORE SERVING

In a medium mixing bowl prepare the pistachio or vanilla pudding mix according to package directions, *except* use the 1¾ cups milk. Cover the surface of the pudding with clear plastic wrap; chill in the *refrigerator*.

Meanwhile, for chocolate sauce, in a 4-cup glass measure combine the milk chocolate pieces and evaporated milk. In the *microwave oven* cook, uncovered, on high power for 4 to 4½ minutes or till the mixture is smooth and slightly thickened, stirring twice during cooking. Cover the surface of the sauce with clear plastic wrap; chill in the *refrigerator*.

20 MINUTES BEFORE SERVING

Spoon *half* of the chilled pistachio or vanilla pudding into 4 parfait glasses. Spoon *half* of the chocolate sauce atop pudding layer. Repeat layers with remaining pudding and chocolate sauce. Sprinkle each serving with chopped almonds, walnuts, or peanuts. Makes 4 servings.

HALIBUT WITH SHERRY SAUCE

3 stalks celery, cut into 2x½-inch strips
1 medium carrot, cut into 2x½-inch strips
2 tablespoons water
⅓ cup water
⅓ cup dry sherry
1½ teaspoons instant chicken bouillon granules
2 orange slices
4 frozen halibut steaks, thawed
½ cup light cream *or* milk
1 tablespoon cornstarch
1 tablespoon snipped parsley

40 MINUTES BEFORE SERVING

In a 12x7½x2-inch nonmetal baking dish combine the celery strips, carrot strips, and the 2 tablespoons water; cover with vented clear plastic wrap. In the *microwave oven* cook on high power for 8 to 9 minutes or till tender, giving dish a half-turn once during cooking. Remove and drain vegetables.

In the same baking dish combine the ⅓ cup water, the dry sherry, chicken bouillon granules, and orange slices. Arrange the thawed halibut steaks in baking dish, placing thicker portions toward outside of dish; cover with waxed paper. Micro-cook on high for 6 to 8 minutes or till the fish flakes easily when tested with a fork, giving the dish a half-turn once during cooking.

10 MINUTES BEFORE SERVING

Transfer the fish to a serving platter, reserving the cooking liquid. Arrange the vegetables around the fish; keep warm.

For sauce, strain the reserved cooking liquid into a 1½-quart saucepan. On the *range top* gently boil liquid till reduced to ⅓ cup. Combine light cream or milk and cornstarch. Stir the cornstarch mixture and parsley into the saucepan. Cook and stir till thickened and bubbly. Cook and stir for 2 minutes more. Pour some of the sauce over fish and vegetables; pass remaining sauce. Makes 4 servings.

DINNER MENU

Monterey Spaghetti Pie

Avocado-Spinach Salad

Pineapple Yogurt Dessert

Beverage

AVOCADO-SPINACH SALAD

¼ cup salad oil
3 tablespoons lime *or* lemon juice
1 tablespoon snipped fresh basil *or*
    1 teaspoon dried basil, crushed
1 teaspoon sugar
½ teaspoon paprika
¼ teaspoon salt
6 cups torn fresh spinach
1 medium avocado, seeded, peeled, halved crosswise, and sliced
1 11-ounce can mandarin orange sections, drained

2 HOURS BEFORE SERVING

For dressing, in a screw-top jar combine salad oil, lime or lemon juice, basil, sugar, paprika, and salt. Cover tightly and shake well to mix. Chill in the *refrigerator*. (*Or*, prepare ahead and chill up to 24 hours.)

20 MINUTES BEFORE SERVING

In a salad bowl combine the spinach, avocado, and mandarin orange sections. Shake dressing again; pour over salad; toss gently to coat. Makes 6 servings.

PINEAPPLE YOGURT DESSERT

1 8-ounce can crushed pineapple (juice pack)
¾ cup orange juice
1 envelope unflavored gelatin
1 8-ounce carton pineapple yogurt
1 egg white
3 orange slices, halved (optional)

24 HOURS BEFORE SERVING

Drain the crushed pineapple, reserving ¼ cup juice; set drained pineapple aside. In a 2-cup glass measure combine the reserved pineapple juice, the orange juice, and unflavored gelatin. In the *microwave oven* cook the gelatin mixture, uncovered, on high power for 2 to 2½ minutes or till gelatin is dissolved, stirring once during cooking.

Stir the gelatin mixture into pineapple yogurt; stir in drained pineapple. Cover and chill the mixture in the *refrigerator* about 2 hours or till consistency of unbeaten egg whites (partially set).

In a mixing bowl beat egg white on high speed of electric mixer till stiff peaks form (tips stand straight). Fold the beaten egg white into the partially set yogurt mixture. Cover and chill in the *refrigerator* about 1 hour more or till mixture can be mounded.

Spoon the pineapple mixture into 6 dessert dishes or parfait glasses. Chill the desserts in the *refrigerator*.

5 MINUTES BEFORE SERVING

If desired, garnish each serving with an orange slice half. Makes 6 servings.

MONTEREY SPAGHETTI PIE

6 ounces spaghetti
2 tablespoons butter *or* margarine
2 beaten eggs
¼ cup grated Parmesan cheese
1 pound ground beef
½ cup chopped onion
1 8-ounce can red kidney beans, drained
1 7½-ounce can tomatoes, cut up
1 6-ounce can tomato paste
¼ cup chopped pitted ripe olives
2 tablespoons chopped canned green chili peppers
¼ teaspoon sugar
¼ teaspoon ground cumin
½ cup shredded Monterey Jack cheese
¼ cup crushed tortilla chips

50 MINUTES BEFORE SERVING

On the *range top,* in a saucepan cook the spaghetti according to package directions; drain (you should have about 3 cups). Stir the butter or margarine into hot spaghetti; stir in the beaten eggs and grated Parmesan cheese. Form the spaghetti mixture into a "crust" in a greased 10-inch pie plate.

Meanwhile, in a 1½-quart nonmetal casserole combine the ground beef and onion. In the *microwave oven* cook, covered, on high power about 5 minutes or till meat is no longer pink and onion is tender. Drain off fat.

Stir kidney beans, *undrained* tomatoes, tomato paste, chopped olives, chili peppers, sugar, and cumin into meat mixture. Micro-cook, covered, on high about 2 minutes or till heated through.

30 MINUTES BEFORE SERVING

Turn the meat mixture into the spaghetti crust. Cover edges with foil. Bake in the *conventional oven* at 350° about 20 minutes or till heated through. Sprinkle with the shredded Monterey Jack cheese and crushed tortilla chips; bake about 5 minutes more or till cheese is melted. Makes 6 servings.